The Good Parent Workbook

PROVEN PARENTING TIPS TO PREVENT AND ADDRESS
ANXIETY IN CHILDREN

Lori Olson, M.S., LCMHC, LMHC, CCHT

The Good Parent Workbook

Proven Parenting Tips to Prevent and Address Anxiety in Children

A stage-of-development approach to parenting

For parents, practitioners and others who care for and love children

Lori Olson, M.S., LCMHC, LMHC, CCHT

First Published by

Burgerbread Press

Burgerbread Press
50 Pleasant Street
Concord, NH 03301

This book is dedicated to my sisters, Donna Hamilton and Deborah Olson, in gratitude for their helping hands, listening ears and playful hearts.

Must Read Before Accessing and Listening to the Hypnotic Guided Imagery Audio Sessions

Warning and Information

The audio components of this workbook are hypnotic in nature. Never listen to the guided imagery audio recordings while operating any sort of machinery, driving a car, walking or interacting in any place that requires you to be alert. These are best listened to while comfortably positioned in a safe place with eyes closed.

While in a hypnotic trance, you will not be a sleep. This means that you can freely open your eyes and respond to anything in your environment that warrants your immediate attention or impacts your safety. You are fully capable of moving your body, should you desire to do so, to be more comfortable. You are also fully capable of opening your eyes, and ending trance if for any reason you desire to end the session. If you are tired and do fall asleep, the words of this hypnotic session will have no impact on you as there is no such thing as sleep learning.

Transcripts of the audio sessions are available in Appendix A along with the links for the hypnotic guided imagery audio recordings. They are available in order to provide transparency. Listeners can rule out concerns about "hidden agendas".

The reader will find that the hypnotic guided imagery scripts follow standard hypnosis protocol. The initial section or the "induction" helps the listener to narrow and direct focus. The body of the audio sessions provide direct and indirect suggestions to help the listener reflect upon the theme of the recording; i.e. building life skills, setting boundaries and making positive personal change. There is a post-hypnotic suggestion near the end of each audio session to increase the likelihood that the lessons in each particular session will be appropriately used in life. The last segment of each session has an invitation to end the focused-state and re-orient from trance.

The style of these hypnotic guided imagery sessions is "permission-based". This means that it primarily invites listeners to engage their imaginations to make their own meaning of the material presented. The goal is to work with the natural neuroplasticity that everyone has (see Appendix B) to facilitate change. Even when metaphors are used, the listener may always "go off" and enjoy whatever imagery or thoughts that are "served up" and make meaning that personally rings true.

Hypnotic guided imagery is not a "cure" for anything (Yapko, 2012). For many people, it is a powerful tool that facilitates learning (or unlearning as is appropriate to the case). It helps people make the changes they need and want. It is powerful when the listener engages in Hildegard's wonderful "believed in imagination" (Yapko, 2012). However, it has little value when a listener is focused on searching for "tricks being used".

It is unlikely that you will experience the same degree of focus when you simply read through the transcripts; so reading alone is less likely to produce hypnotic experience. However, you must remember that a hypnotic trance does not require relaxation or closed eyes. It simply requires a strong selective focus and absorption of attention. This means that people can and do generate trance while reading (e.g. getting "lost" in a good book).

Instructions for accessing the hypnotic guided imagery sessions can be found in Appendix A.

These 3 hypnotic guided imagery sessions are for the express use of individuals who have purchased this workbook. Any other use is unauthorized. Practitioners who are interested in utilizing the audio sessions with clients (individually or in group sessions or workshops) must first gain written permission to do so. Requests for permission or more information can be directed to Burgerbread Press, 50 Pleasant Street, Concord, NH 03301.

Table of Contents

Preface

Imagine that you could become the type of parent you always hoped and wanted to be. The dream parent would model problem-solving competence to children. Such an ideal parent would also be able to guide children, in an age-appropriate way, so children developed impulse control; became emotionally well adjusted; developed self-discipline; became trustworthy, honest and responsible citizens and most importantly, loved, honored and appreciated all the hard work made by the (sacrificing) parent. Sound impossible?

It is highly probable that, at this point, you are already very skeptical that any parent could do half as much (except for the sacrifice). You might be thinking, "All I want is for my kids to be happy" (global thinking; failure to compartmentalize). "After all, kids are tougher these days and the world is scary and worse than ever and full of all kinds of impossible challenges; e.g. sexting, bullying, substance abuse (more global thinking, externalization and catastrophizing). What if my child is bullied? What if my child gets sucked in by negative peers? What if…What if….What if my child doesn't get into a good college"? (Examples of rumination and catastrophizing). After all, a parent might be thinking that a child "gets all the breaks" coming from that part of town and no one ever succeeds from this part (all or nothing thinking; victim-like thinking; failure to create a logical sequence toward a future vision).

Hopefully, the previous hypothetical statements (and descriptions of the dysfunctional anxiety producing nature of the statements) pique your curiosity and get you wondering whether being a "good parent" involves more (and how much more?) than just being lucky enough to get kids with good temperaments (who also seem to succeed in avoiding bully types and live in the right place at the right time and other such things that are pretty much beyond one's control).

And while it is truly safe to say that the world is indeed a challenging place that is far too often unsafe (even treacherous), it is also safe to say that raising "good kids" is more than a stroke of luck. It is also not a matter of parents having to be perfect or even doing everything mostly right most of the time. The reality is that the good or

14

"dream" parent (in the opening paragraph), only needs to be "good enough".

That's right. The "good enough parent" (modified from Winnicott's "good enough mother" description, 1964) is actually all that is needed to yield the type of results described in paragraph one. Surely, "good enough parent" needs to be clarified. It does not mean being "highly motivated but relatively clueless" and it also does not just mean being "a good person". Being a "good enough parent" means taking the time and energy to learn developmentally appropriate parenting principles and deliver them in a consistently human way (which means fallible and loving).

Children do not need "perfect parents" since such parents end up modeling standards that cannot be "lived up to". This leads to all sorts of ill-will and trouble. Rather children benefit from seeing parents, who are fallible yet open and comfortable enough to model problem-solving and also model recovery from and repair of mistakes.

When parents are mindful of what children are actually capable of learning during each of the various stages of child development, children can be helped to develop life skills that enable them in many ways; this includes being better able to navigate the challenges presented by the world. When parents help children gain important life skill competencies, children will have a better chance to lead truly authentic lives and will feel empowered to make choices that help them actualize their goals. Additionally and very importantly, children raised by "good enough parents" will learn skills that will decrease their vulnerability to developing anxiety and depression. Life skill knowledge will render protection from childhood through adulthood (even though anxiety and depression are conditions that are rapidly increasing around the world).

This is what the parenting skills in this workbook will help you accomplish; it is no small task but extraordinarily worth-while. Your diligence in learning and applying these parenting skills can lead to increased emotional intimacy in your family; this means your family will be better able to provide safe harbor in any storm that life creates. This is truly wonderful.

And why is learning the skills "no small task"? The answer is simply that as humans, we "get in our own way". Hence, the reason that this workbook also provides directions for downloading 3 guided imagery audio sessions. These downloads are hypnotic in nature and are "short cut" aids to help parents think about some skills that may have gotten sidetracked due to "bumps" that occurred in their own childhood journeys. The goal is to fortify parents so that less gets in the way of being fully present, patient or sensitive to a child's developmental needs (Please see the Appendix B to learn more about guided imagery and hypnosis).

Anxiety is a serious life-interfering condition (and can be a very debilitating condition) it can be prevented and reduced by using the parenting principles in this book. Prevention of anxiety is important for its own sake and also because childhood anxiety is a very strong predictor that major depression may occur during young adulthood (Yapko, 2009). Once a person has experienced depression, the risk factor for future episodes is significantly higher.

Despite, this dire news, there is good news. The human brain is very resilient. Decades of research in neuroscience tells us that thought patterns and behavior patterns can and do change (Siegel, 2010). Change requires learning new skills and applying them long enough and consistently enough to create new neuro-patterns. However, change is much harder to make when strong thought and behavior patterns have already been instilled. This is why it is so very important and useful to help children develop the right skills from the start (or as soon as possible).

However, you must know that no matter the age, people can (and do) change. The goal of this workbook is to invite you to look at parenting (and yourself) in a whole new way so you can join in the effort to make this world a calmer, more responsive and better problem–solving place...one kid at a time...one parent at a time.

Overview

What will this course teach?

This course will teach you highly effective parenting skills that:

- Prevent the development of destructive parent-child power-struggles

- Reduce or even eliminate any existing parent-child power-struggles

- Create more harmonious family relationships

- Help you more effectively instill your family values in your children

- Help children build skills to prevent anxiety and depression from starting or deepening

- Help reduce levels of existing anxiety and depression (this workbook will not replace any professional help that may be needed)

The parenting methods in this workbook are simple and straightforward. The hardest part, for most parents, is actually having enough self-awareness to consistently implement the skills stated. Utilizing the audio downloads (see Appendix A for instructions) that accompany this workbook will help parents fine tune self-awareness. The recorded sessions are designed to help with boundary setting and other life skills such as relieving defensiveness that may interfere with good parenting. This auditory portion accompanies the workbook so that parents are better able to put aside personal issues of the past and become more responsive parents.

The good news is that the methods describe in this workbook for parenting are relatively simple; even though the reasons as to why these methods works are substantial. The influence that using these methods can have on your children is *significant*. However, and once again, the results depend on how consistently parents implement this system. *It is important to remember that it is not necessary to be perfect*, (Szymanski, 2011) as a matter of fact, striving toward perfection is discouraged. It is simply necessary to demonstrate commitment, flexibility and willingness to make repairs when mistakes are made (more on this later). Well respected studies (Yapko, 2009) show that childhood anxiety is a major precursor to adult depression. These studies also show that effective communication and coping skills; emotional regulation; distress tolerance; problem-solving and impulse control are essential to prevent it. There is much evidence that these types of life skills contribute to healthier and more resilient lives.

The methods in this workbook are based on many decades of evidence-based research from child development (Winnicott, 1964); trauma (Van der Kolk, 2014; Heller & Lapierre, 2012; Arnold & Fisch, 2011; Levine, 2010); psychotherapy (Greenberg & Watson, 2005); attachment (Booth & Jernberg, 2010); mindfulness (Hayes, 2005); family systems (Sweezy, 2013); brain neuroplasticity studies (Siegel, 2010) and more. Much of this information is so commonly used in therapeutic sessions that it becomes hard to separate the information and point to original sources. The material in this book is not intended to be represented as "an original parenting system"; rather, it is a compilation of the many tried and true methods that I have used and recommended to community mental health and private practice clients. The goal is to empower parents and to help stop the "contagion" (Yapko, 2009) of anxiety and depression in children. The reference list at the end of this book will help readers who want to find more in-depth sources about this material since this workbook is intended to be a brief, practical guide.

Who is this for?

These parenting skills are useful for guiding children ages 2-25.

When you use the parenting skills in this workbook, you will be guiding your children (even when you are unaware that you are doing so) so they can:

- Develop greater frustration tolerance and impulse control

- Accept limits and behave responsibly

- Authentically unfold and develop into the unique people they were meant to be

- Feel safe to come to you with their problems

- Build healthy ties with family members and develop pro-social skills

- Discipline self so as to be able to create goals and make progress towards completing those goals

- Learn to be confident and effective problem-solvers

- Learn to accept feedback as well as learn from mistakes

- Develop a healthy self-esteem

- Become a person that lives by the values of your family

- Develop an internal sense of accountability

- Have skills that prevent and reduce vulnerability to anxiety and depression

Workbook Exercises - Course Overview

Name at least 5 parenting skills that you hope to get out of this course.

_____

_____

_____

_____

_____

_____

_____

_____

_____

_____

_____

_____

_____

_____

_____

_____

_____

_____

_____

Organization of Workbook

With these goals in mind, this course is divided in a way to better inform you about why the system works. You do not have to commit the "whys" to memory to use the parenting skills. You do not have to be a memorized "textbook" or become a parenting "expert". The parenting skills that you will use are actually few in number; however, they need to be consistently implemented so as to be able to foster and develop the underlying principles. The brief presentation of underlying principles is meant to fortify you and help you stay on course; especially when you are challenged by the opinions of less-informed family members, friends and other advice-givers.

The course, thus, has the following informational parts to support The Framework (in part 8):

1. Introduction
    a. What this Course Will Do
    b. What this Course Will Not Do
    c. Why this Course Works

2. Must Know Foundational Principles
    a. Parenting Principles
    b. Summary of Principles

3. Child Development Basics
    a. Attachment
    b. Terrible Twos
    c. Pre-Operational Thinking
    d. Magical Thinking to Adolescence
    e. Teenage Years
    f. Young Adults

4. Communication Basics
    a. Obstacles Blocking Effective Communication

Introduction

First, let's take a look at what this course will/will not do for you as a parent and secondly, take a look at why it works. Thirdly, we will very briefly touch on the types of success these methods have over a wide range of circumstances. Lastly, we will consider the science that supports the parenting framework described through the remainder of the workbook.

What this Course **Will Do**

- Teach a framework for interacting with your children to help them more effectively learn and adhere to your family's value system

- Help you eliminate power-struggles which are destructive and are strong predictors of oppositional children and/or fearful children (depending on the temperament of the child and other factors in the home environment and social setting)

- Help you retain parental authority

- Help you be a more effective guide to help children develop confidence and competence in problem-solving

- Help you recognize where, when and how to set limits with children

- Help you enforce limits and consequences in a way that fosters growth of children

- Help you model and teach life skills that prevent and reduce anxiety and depression

What It **Will Not** Do

- This course will not replace your family's value system

- It will not tell you what rules to make in your house

- It is not about how to be a friend or buddy to your child

- It is not about "making" everyone happy

- It is not about helping you win a family "popularity contest"

Workbook Exercises - What this Course Will and Will Not Do

Name 3 parenting issues that this course will help you address –

_____
_____
_____

Name 3 parenting concerns that this course will not impact –

_____
_____
_____

Write your pre-workbook thoughts about anxiety and depression; what contributes to and how they can be addressed.

_____
_____
_____

Why This Course Works

The methods in this course are based on sound psychological principles which take into consideration the following:

- Child's developmental age and needs

- The way children learn

- The way children develop a sense of responsibility

- The way children learn to control impulses

- The way parents can most effectively communicate to children so that children will understand

- Life skills people need to effectively and flexibly deal with issues that "normal" (and challenging) lives typically have

Because this system takes into consideration the above mentioned points, the parenting framework offered in this workbook, is useful and practical for a wide range of parenting styles and family situations. It can be successfully used in any situation or place where people need to provide guidance to children.

Wide Range of Applications

This framework can be flexibly used in: correctional facilities, community mental health centers; schools; parenting centers and workshops; and private therapeutic counseling practice. Consider the following examples from this author's professional experiences:

Oppositional youth, ages 13-18, in correctional and residential facilities benefited. When repeat offenders in a juvenile justice system, who initially refused to participate in group therapy were *actively listened to and allowed to collaboratively set goals,* (both of these methods are described in upcoming sections), they began to interact in more positive and pro-social ways. This included holding each other accountable when antisocial behavior flared up. Youth, who had been identified as "difficult" themselves, began to recognize and call out the negative and counterproductive behaviors of other less aware group members; e.g. by saying such things as "Hey…be a positive youth". Group conversation became more active, honest and meaningful to these group members. Prior to using this framework, the youth were angry, cynical and refused to engage.

Single teen mothers were able to *positively influence responsiveness of their children* (and ultimately influence IQ). Studies (Siegel, 2010) show that talking, singing and interacting in a developmentally appropriate manner with a child, positively influences that child's abilities in many ways; these include: increasing a child's ability to emotionally regulate (socially as well as ability to self-soothe) and increasing a child's capacity for verbal and other types of learning (ultimately helping a child to do better in school and life). Singing and positively interacting with children prevents the "pruning" of unused nervous (i.e. unstimulated and under stimulated) pathways in the child's brain and increases a child's brain organization. All of the positive interaction contributes to better emotional regulation (i.e. helping the child learn to settle down). This creates a wonderful foundation for learning.

Family conflict subsides when parents provide safe and predictable limits and consequences. When a safe and predictable home environment exists, children begin to become accountable for their actions and develop good self-esteem. This is in place of inadvertently shaming children when poor choices are made. Instead, children are helped to learn from their mistakes. In my experiences, real-life parents repeatedly demonstrated that even children, who had been labeled as "oppositional", began to change when those parents *lovingly and firmly* enforced rules which had *collaboratively* been made with their children (under the limits, guidance and values of parents). This occurred and continues to occur across a wide variety of family value systems.

Based on Research

More than thirty years of sophisticated studies (Wilson, 2004, 2011) in neuroscience have repeatedly demonstrated that humans are "socially wired" and emotions play an enormous part in organizing the wiring (see Appendix F).

An early and now famous neuroscience study resulted in the discovery of "mirror neurons" in the brain (Wilson, 2004). During an experiment in the 1980s, Italian scientists were seeking to map neural pathways in the brains of Rhesus monkeys. Much to their surprise, the scientists discovered, that monkeys, observing the actions of other monkeys, showed activation responses *in the same areas of their brains* as in the brains of the monkeys actively performing the task. These mirror neurons, as they came to be called, also exist in humans. The concept explains why yawns are contagious, and people cry or laugh more easily when observing others doing a particular behavior (even when the actions occur in a movie).

Brain Navigation

Further studies show that human brains are "mapped" (Siegel, 2010) by the interactions babies have with primary caregivers. This happens from the moment of birth and throughout childhood. This means parents play a crucial role in shaping the way children organize the way they see and experience the world. This includes seeing the world as a safe, or hostile or fearful place. It influences whether the child develops confidence in being able to problem-solve or whether the child takes a more complacent or even victim style approach to the world.

Hebb's concept of "what fires together, wires together" is another generally accepted brain science principle (Arnold & Fisch, 2011; Booth & Jernberg, 2010; Siegel, 2010). In other words, when sights, sounds, smells, and sensations are repeatedly stimulated at the same time ("fire together"), a neuro-pattern develops that can be triggered later on; even when only one of the components fires. Patterns are usually more "deeply" wired when a strong emotion occurred at the time of the "firing". Thus, early childhood memories of upset can be wired together and triggered later on; seeming at times, inexplicable. Examples of triggers include: a tone of voice, a particular facial expression, the sound of the rain or a particular smell and so many other overt or subtle signals. In the case of trauma, such sensations (sight, sound, touch, smell, taste) can trigger "flashback" memories.

The Importance of Physical and Emotional Safety

This brief discussion points to the incredible importance of creating physically and emotionally safe environments. The goal is to create the best possible environments so children can explore and acquire the necessary life skills to become authentic and competent. This means being true to one's self; rather than have an identity burdened by "should". It also means developing the capacity to be flexible and resourceful problem-solvers.

It is important to note that physically and emotionally safe environments *are not dependent* upon the number of material goods that parents can or do provide to children. This is because emotionally and physically safe environments are richer than environments that defensively use material goods to create or regulate relationships. This means that parents do not have to worry about keeping up with the latest trends or trendiest neighbors.

It is also important to remember that there is no such thing as a "perfect" world. Children can and do thrive, when they are equipped with good, solid life skills. These life skills will be discussed throughout this workbook. Children will benefit when parents teach and model these skills to them. Parents will benefit when they use the skills in their personal and professional lives; especially when, there are challenges that need to be overcome.

Child Development

The parenting skills outlined in this course are not only based on the neuroscience principles mentioned but also on child development principles. The skills described in the course will help you create emotionally safe, predictable and *age-appropriate* environments for your children.

The skills are straightforward and practical. They are simple to learn; however, they may be challenging for parents to put into action. *This may happen when parents have preconceived and erroneous notions about what children can do; given the child's stage of development.* It may also be challenging to put into action when parents have entrenched habits that resist change. This means that once the skills are learned, it may be challenging for parents to utilize the skills consistently. But don't worry. And remember...this is not about being perfect. The audio download portion of this workbook will help you boost your own life skills.

Parenting that addresses children's developmental needs is about:

- Modeling competence in problem-solving and being appropriately flexible

- Creating a home environment that is safe and predictable

- Setting age-appropriate limits and consequences

- Providing unconditional love even when firmly disciplining children with consequences; because this is what children need and want

- Being emotionally accessible and appropriate

27

- Modeling and teaching life skills to prevent and reduce experiences of anxiety and depression

Workbook Exercises – Why this Course Works

What is the major psychological basis upon which this course rests?

_____

_____

_____

What is the concept of "what fires together, wires together" mean? How does that inform parenting choices?

_____

_____

_____

_____

_____

_____

What is a "mirror neuron"? How does this influence child development?

_____

_____

_____

Describe the concept and importance of mind "mapping".

_____

_____

_____

Summary of Why this Course Works

The parenting principles in this course are *based on well-accepted empirical research about child development, attachment, anxiety and depression, social regulation, neuroscience and hypnosis. The methods that arise from this research are clinically supported.*

Parenting and child development principles will be discussed throughout the course *to increase awareness and understanding*; however, the reader needs to be aware that simply using the parenting framework as outlined in this workbook is sufficient. The workbook exercises are included to help the information "stick".

Must-Know Foundational Principles

Parenting Principles

Here are some must-know foundational principles. Remembering these principles will help you stay committed to learning and using the parenting skills taught in this course.

- **Children's emotional and physical wellbeing depends on the care of parents.** Children's very survival depends on it. This means that even if things have gotten off track, underneath it all, *nothing is more pleasing to a child than to be in right relationship with the parent(s)*.

- **Children are not capable of manipulating until they have more sophisticated brains** (in later teenage years). This means that when children consistently misbehave to get something, *they have been inadvertently taught* that such behavior achieves their desired end(s). This means that parents need to figure out how they are *accidentally* training the child to do this problem behavior and, then of course, they need to figure out how to stop teaching it.

- **Children are not "little adults" and should not be treated as if they are.** This means that *no matter how smart they appear to be, they still have child brains*.

  A child's brain is not emotionally mature. A child's brain does not have the executive capacity to reason and think in complex ways (the human brain does not become an adult brain until age 25). The brains of children are simply not as physically, emotionally, or cognitively complex as those of adults. It is *due to biology and not due to any deficit or fault of the child*. Human brains take 25 years to develop. It is an unfair burden to expect a child to act in a way that is beyond his/her developmental age (more about this later). For now, it is enough to consider that children will do anything to please a parent; even take on the burden of appearing older than they really are. This is not to say that you do not have to set limits and have expectations of compliance. It just means you must *set realistic expectations that take into consideration the child's developmental capabilities*.

- **Your family is not a democracy.** *Children should not have equal say with parents.* This undermines parental authority and accidentally trains children to negotiate with parents. This sets up *power struggles*. Power struggles lead to oppositional children (parents must also not be tyrants or doormats as these contribute to power struggles too; more on this later).

- **Parental and adult matters should be kept separate from children**. Parents should present a unified front. This means parents need to work out differences without children present; this is true, even, when parents are divorced. In the case of divorced parents with 2 different households, each parent/household can have separate rules, but it benefits children when parents use the same parenting skills framework provided in this course (at the minimum of keeping parental and adult matters separate from the children).

- **Parents do not have to be perfect and neither do children.** This is an unrealistic standard which leads to fear of failure; fear of trying (in case a mistake is made); fear of loss of approval or love; and fear of being one's authentic self (since "I might not be good enough"). Rather than striving to be perfect, people need to be resilient. This means have the skills to tolerate frustration and disappointment and still problem solve. Children need to learn accountability. Parents need to model effective coping and other life skills to use when facing life's stressors.

- **Respect, appreciation and trust are earned.** These qualities are not obtained by parental demanding on or coercing and shaming of children. They are earned when a parent (or any person) behaves in a manner that is consistent with the values he/she professes. Demanding respect from a child just because a parent can "pull rank" will only result in a child giving "lip service". It is better to model behavior worthy of respect/appreciation/trust and set/enforce appropriate limits and consequences around a child's behaviors. Children will respect, appreciate and trust parents when they are mature enough to grasp and understand such complex and abstract emotions. These feelings will naturally grow in children when parents consistently use sound and loving parenting practices. Note: Do not confuse the feeling of respect with disrespectful behaviors (behaviors do need limits and consequences placed around them).

Summary of Principles

- Nothing is more pleasing to a child than to be in right relationship with the parent(s).

- When children consistently misbehave to get something, they have been inadvertently taught that a particular behavior achieves the desired end; i.e. to get their needs met.

- No matter how smart children appear to be, they still have child brains (which means lacking in complex thinking and emotionally immature).

- Children should not have equal say with parents (this invites negotiations which lead to power struggles).

- Parental and adult matters should be kept separate from children.

- Parents do not have to be perfect and neither do children; people need to learn resilience and accountability.

- Respect and trust are earned.

Workbook Exercises – Foundational Principles

True or False

Children of all ages can learn to and do manipulate adults to get what they want.

Children must respect and appreciate parents because parents are older and know more.

Smart children can be treated as little adults because they are clever enough to understand.

Parents can be held to a different standard than children; i.e. children must "Do as I say and not as I do".

Children have rights and therefore must have equal say with parents.

All children are self-absorbed and do not want to please parents.

All people need to learn accountability and resiliency.

Child Development Basics

The human brain needs time to develop structural complexity in order to support intellectual and emotional growth (Arnold & Fisch, 2011; Singer & Revenson, 1996; Piaget, 1950). It is a huge mistake to suppose that a bright child has emotional capacities beyond his/her developmental years. Statements such as "8 years old going on 20" point more to parenting style than to advancement in child development. It is more likely that such a child does not have parents who set age-appropriate limits, has parents who use power-struggle tactics, or is parentified to meet external expectations that are inappropriate for the age of the child.

The following sections will briefly touch on "highlights" from the major stages of child development (see the reference section for more in-depth resources on this topic).

Attachment

Secure attachment is all about feeling safe and connected to parent(s) and other caregivers (Bowlby, 1988). Creating secure attachment is extremely important as it allows a child to feel comfortable enough to take risks to explore the world and grow. How is this accomplished? Parents need to:

- **Respond to a child's cries and needs in a timely and loving manner**. As a child develops during the first year, parents need to "read" the baby in order to know how quickly and how much to respond. Besides responding to the baby's needs for sleep, food and cleanliness, this includes learning how much to stimulate a child and when to stop stimulating the child. This means recognizing when a child's immature nervous system will become overstimulated. Parents also need to help the baby learn how to settle in and how to self-soothe. All these tasks require parents to become attuned to the baby (Siegel, 2010). Attunement is an important skill (Van der Kolk, 2014). It is accomplished by careful and attentive trial and error. Remembering that a baby's neural network is still very primitive will help you understand that a baby simply cannot manipulate you or be spoiled by you. On the contrary, your attentive responses will powerfully stimulate your baby's brain to develop nervous pathways that will help your baby regulate and self-soothe.

- **Be a "mirror" to the baby**. Cooing and smiling to a baby activates brain neurons and begins to shape the way the baby "sees" self and the world. This is another extremely important step to help "map" neural pathways in your baby's brain. When you act as a "mirror" to your baby, you are helping your baby make order out of the chaos that comes with the immature newborn's unstructured brain. Mirroring helps build neural circuits and prevents unnecessary "pruning" of brain cells. Pruning happens due to "the use it or lose it" efficiency of the brain.

It is important for you to know, that even if only one parent (in the case of divorce or otherwise) acts in a manner to create a secure attachment style, it will have a major influence on the wellbeing of your child. It is also important to know that even when children have less than secure attachments, strong overall parenting skills will help a lot (see Appendix G for more information about attachment)

Workbook Exercise – Attachment

Name at least 3 things that parents can do to create secure attachments in children:

_____
_____
_____

_____
_____
_____

True or False

Secure attachment will make a baby become too dependent.

Meeting a baby's needs too quickly will hinder the baby's self-soothing skill development.

Not meeting a baby's needs soon enough will have no impact, since babies do not remember much.

A secure attachment style will help a child feel free to explore the world.

Parents need to practice attuning to their baby to understand the temperament nuances particular to that child.

Terrible Twos

The age of two (give or take some months) typically marks a major milestone of development for children (Piaget, 1964). It is unfortunate that such an important milestone has been dubbed "terrible twos". This negative label creates many parental misunderstandings about the capabilities and motivations of children. This name leads people to think of a two year old child as "willful", "bratty" and "manipulative".

These labels are inappropriate and very disconnected from what is really going on in a two year old's quickly developing yet still very immature brain. It would be much better if parents would celebrate the landmark "no" that is uttered by two year olds and understand what it really means. It means the child has a sense of self as being a separate person. This little separate person is chock full of opinions. This is a big leap forward from the unstructured brain capacities of a newborn baby. Later, in this workbook, when the topic of setting and defending healthy emotional boundaries is discussed, the importance of being able to say "no" will be looked at even more closely.

Primitive Capacity to Regulate

Even though, this stage of development is a landmark, it is still just a very early marker in child development. Although the child has a better sense of self as a person and is full of opinions, the child still has very little knowledge of language and virtually no awareness of what to do when tides of emotion ebb and flow. Hence, it is very easy for two year olds to become emotionally dysregulated (includes experiencing positive or negative emotions; e.g. overstimulated by joy or anger). In order to help children learn how to cope, parents need to continue to "map" experiences for children. Consider the following scenario.

Compare a parent who puts a rough hand on a fitful two year old, yanks the child or brusquely yells at the child to the behaviors of a parent who first gives the child a calming hug. Perhaps, upon initial glance, the first parent may appear to be a "no nonsense" type of disciplinarian. The second parent may at first appear too indulgent.

However, there is more than meets the eye. The first parent will end up adding to the emotional chaos experienced by the child. The child of the first parent will also be confused by the hostile behavior stemming from someone who is supposed to provide protection.

The parent who first seeks to calm the child, may initially look "weak" or indulgent, but ultimately, will have *set the stage to be much more successful* in setting and enforcing limits. This is because the child is provided with the opportunity to calm down. Because the child can be allowed to feel safe, it is much more likely that the child can absorb what the parent says to set limits.

Even if the child has a hard time settling down, parents can use it as an opportunity to "map" the child's anger, frustration, disappointment and so forth. It becomes a matter of saying to the child: "Seems like you are angry that you can't have a lollipop...let's hug... so you can calm down.... let's see what else you can do to help you calm down".

If the child still acts the feeling out in an aggressive way, then it is an opportunity to continue to help the child identify the feeling and *consider other courses of action*. When bad behaviors occur that continue to overwhelm the child's capacity to regulate, (e.g. throwing self on floor), a time out lesson may be required. In general, children do best when they are told about limits and consequences *in advance* of the need to enforce them (more on this later).

On the other hand, the parent, who yells at or yanks a child, will further flood the child with negative emotion and will further dysregulate the child. This will leave the child frightened, confused and left to immature emotional devices to survive (e.g. striking people; yelling; throwing self on the ground or throwing things).

The child is left without any sense of what the flood of feelings meant (e.g. anger, sad, frustration) because no one was able to identify and interpret it for the child. No one was present to help the child calm down or help the child learn other ways to deal with the flood of emotions. Additionally, the child will not get a sense of feeling loved during such times. Negative emotional floods are terrifying all on their own. They are especially disconcerting when they also precipitate parental disapproval and disconnection. Two year olds have a very hard time tolerating shame. It is so very difficult for children to feel emotionally separated from their caregivers. Shame is psychologically disorganizing (Arnold & Fisch, 2011). Children will always fare better when a loving parent helps them calm down; as this enables limits to be heard and enforced.

Workbook Exercise – Terrible Twos

Is a two year old capable of manipulating other people?

_____

_____

_____

What is the significance of saying "no" for a two year old? Does it mean that the child is willful?

_____

_____

_____

What must a parent consider when a two year old is behaving poorly?

_____

_____

_____

_____

_____

_____

Pre-Operational Thinking

The two year old brain transitions from an infant's sensorimotor stage of development (Piaget, 1964), where thinking is not language based, to pre-operational style of thinking typical of toddlers. The child now thinks in a very literal fashion. Thinking is tied to the actions that occur _at the time. There is no inner symbolic universe_ to "manipulate" since children in this stage of development still have little language and other internal representations. This is important to know.

As a child begins to develop greater language skills and becomes physically more independent, it becomes quite easy to mistakenly think that the child is more capable (emotionally and intellectually) than he/she actually is. This is particularly true for children who are bigger than their peers. Mistaken perceptions about what is and is not developmentally appropriate continue from the "terrible twos" throughout childhood. The typical but erroneous expectation, during this stage of development, is that 3 year olds are capable of understanding the concept of sharing.

To Share or Not to Share

Sharing is a very complex concept for a child. The difficulty of sharing becomes even more apparent when one considers that such a little child *is still making sense* of a notion as basic as being a separate person (with separate opinions and wants). Three year old children are just learning words to label feelings and still have very little ability to regulate negative emotions.

When a three year old child is forced to share, the child may have a meltdown because sharing is too confusing. Sharing also requires having more distress tolerance than three year olds can muster. Certainly children can and need to be introduced to concepts such as sharing; however, the introduction needs to be done in a way that realistically considers what the child can understand and tolerate.

Role Models

Parents can model sharing through actions and also by simply narrating what they are doing. Parents also need to protect children from situations that "force sharing". It is far better to take "preemptive strikes" and make sure that every child has the same or similar toy or food. Children from both sides of the equation; i.e. both the "have" and "have nots", will feel challenged and their perspectives need to be considered.

Strange Logic

There are many ways in which pre-operational thinkers differ from adult brains, adolescents and even older children. Such differences influence how much a pre-operational child understands and interprets the world.

For example, pre-operational thinkers are very narcissistic (i.e. self-absorbed) and have a very hard time shifting perspectives. They think the world is just like them and so they are not yet able to be objective and see the perspective of someone else; i.e. It simply "is" the way the child sees it.

Other qualities include: inability to think of two opposing ideas; ability to concentrate only on one aspect of something at a time; and clumping together unrelated thoughts when attempting to reason. A child might wonder and conclude: "If I think about it and it happens, then I must be at fault". This strange type of logic is the basis for "magical thinking". However, these types of thought patterns are very appropriate for this stage of development. Children will grow out this sort of thinking as they mature and as parents teach age-appropriate limits. These thought patterns cannot be "reasoned away"; *no matter how much or how well a parent attempts to explain.* Children may agree with the parent on the outside; however, their interior experiences will continue to be different.

Workbook Exercise – Pre-Operational Thinking

Can a three year old child truly understand what it means to share?

_____

_____

_____

Should parents spend a lot of time explaining reasons to small children? If so, why? If not, why?

_____

_____

_____

What does "magical thinking" mean?

_____

_____

_____

Magical Thinking to Adolescence

As children continue to emotionally develop, degrees of magical thinking will linger

(Arnold & Fisch, 2011; Bowlby, 1988; Piaget, 1964) until the child begins to develop and mature the executive portions of the brain. Executive development revs up in adolescence and continues to rapidly grow through the teen years and into early adulthood.

Although children increasingly gain greater command of language, and are developing greater emotional regulation and greater impulse control, children up until age 10 or 11, still largely express negative emotions through *restlessness or disruptive behavior*. The choice of parenting skills used during this stage of development will either help or hinder emotional development as children navigate this period.

Childhood Anxiety and Depression

Childhood anxiety and depression are commonly manifested during this stage of development with symptoms that look like: *inattention, poor focus, and irritability*. Unfortunately, many teachers and primary care physicians are much too quick to proclaim "Attention Deficit" or "Bipolar" disorders instead of insisting upon further investigation.

Such misdiagnoses end up frightening parents. Misled parents end up feeling pressured to accept incorrect and harmful "remedies". It is highly recommended that parents take any child "diagnosed", by a teacher or primary care physician, to a qualified mental health professional for further evaluation. It is best if parents have their child re-evaluated before any medication regiment is implemented. However, even when a child is already taking medication and a parent wonders if a misdiagnosis was given, it is prudent to have a qualified mental health professional reevaluate the diagnosis.

In many cases, parents may find that the problem really is a matter of helping their children learn how to improve self-regulation and build life skills. Life skills can help children break dysfunctional thought and behavior patterns.

More Studies

Studies strongly and repeatedly point to the negative impact that dysfunctional thought and behavior patterns have on a person's ability to cope. Dysfunctional patterns that are modeled to and reinforced in children make it more difficult for them to build age-appropriate coping and regulation skills. Dysfunctional patterns hinder the refining of newly budding life skills. This "refining" should take place in the developmental years yet to come, but a poorly laid foundation in the earlier stages, makes this harder to do. Dysfunctional patterns contribute to and exacerbate life skill deficits.

Breaking the Patterns of Dysfunction

Life skill deficits contribute heavily to experiences of anxiety and depression as well as the development of life long patterns of anxiety and depression (Yapko, 2009). Although, this news is very alarming, it is very important to note that these patterns can be broken by people of all ages. It happens when people learn to cope, communicate and function in more effective ways and *bust the anxiety making cycle* (see upcoming section).

In summary, whenever children are incorrectly diagnosed by mental health and non-mental health professionals, it means these children are more likely to be inappropriately treated for conditions they do not actually have. They may be prescribed medications for "disorders" (including anxiety) that would be more effectively addressed by life skill development. This includes: helping children learn distress tolerance; emotional regulation; and effective ways to access, identify and pro-socially communicate their legitimate needs, wants and feelings. Children can be helped and are helped; even when the challenges are great.

Children as Manipulators

Even during this stage of development, children are not capable of being "manipulators". Their brains have not yet begun to develop the complexity needed to genuinely manipulate. During this phase of development, children are very "black and white thinkers". This "all or nothing" perspective, leads children to reach odd conclusions such as: "My parents are fighting and I feel yucky.....I must be yucky"; I am angry at my mother.....I want another mother" and so forth. Depending on the intensity and frequency of the experiences, some of the associated emotions may become enduring and color the child's sense of self.

The Harm in Over-Explaining

Pre-adolescent children still do not have advanced executive centers in their brains and it is a mistake to explain things as if they can understand adult reasons. It is a common and easy mistake to over-explain things to a child in an attempt to be "reasonable and fair". Since children do not fully grasp adult reasons, over-explaining simply encourages children to view themselves as peers to the adult.

Over-explaining by adults also inadvertently encourages children to negotiate. This accidentally leads to the creation of power struggle dynamics. Over-explaining can lead to children feeling discounted, since from the child's perspective, the adult appears to dismiss the child's logic and feelings. Alternatively, it can lead to feelings of entitlement and invite future negotiations whenever the adult ends up "giving in".

It is thus important to note that the poor behaviors seen during the magical thinking phase of childhood are generally behaviors that have been accidentally taught by adults. It is very common for adults to inadvertently use the principle of "cause and effect" to teach children undesirable behaviors; e.g. when the child acts out, the parent gives in and the child achieves the desired outcome. This happens, for example, when parents do not set sufficient limits; feel "guilty", second guess their decisions; train children to negotiate, and engage in power-struggles.

Concrete Thinkers

During the pre-adolescent stage of development, it is important that parents remember not to be "duped" by children who attempt to act beyond their years, as in "I am not afraid of that movie". Remember, developmental stages exist and the tasks of each stage need to be completed.

Pre-adolescent children are still very concrete, all or nothing, magical thinkers. This is a fact of life that needs to be embraced rather than ignored. Ignoring the actual capabilities of children ends up burdening them to be logical beyond their years. A parent who is not mindful of this fact, runs the risk of accidentally elevating children beyond the child's developmental age to "little adult status". This is called parentifying a child. This is hard on children since it robs them of the opportunity to be their natural selves and places unfair, heavy and confusing weight on them.

A good rule to follow during this child development stage, is to keep parental/adult matters separate from children. This means not only keeping children out of adult conversations, but also keeping the adult conversation out of children's earshot.

Workbook Exercise – Magical Thinking

What does it mean to be a "magical thinker"?

_____

_____

_____

What can a parent do to prevent a child from becoming a "little adult"?

_____

_____

_____

What good parenting rule applies in particular to this age of child development?

_____

_____

_____

What signs might a parent observe if a child were suffering from anxiety or depression?

_____

_____

_____

What should a parent do if they suspect a child may have some mental health concerns (including being labeled by teachers and/or a non-mental health professional)?

_____

_____

_____

_____

Teenage Years

The teenage stage of development is a very challenging period for parents and children. This is due to the many and very rapid developmental changes that occur during this time frame. Parents often wonder, "Who is this kid?" and children often echo this sentiment thinking "Who am I?" In the same way the misnomer "terrible twos" discredits the landmark changes that occurred to the infant, teenage years also have a "bad rap". The "bad rap" is when teens are, across the board, deemed to be difficult, sullen, or oppositional by nature. It is far more accurate and productive to think of the teen years in terms of the growth challenges that children face during this time. This better paves the way for thinking about how to help teens navigate the enormous challenges they face.

Many Challenges

Teens simultaneously experience significant physical maturation of their bodies and significant cognitive and emotional and physical growth in their brains. This means that teens not only look different physically, but they feel, think and act differently. It is, no doubt, a more foreign experience to them than it is to their parents (who have already been through this stage).

Hormones Rule

The significant physical, cognitive and emotional changes are driven by hormone fluctuations which contribute to mood swings. The enormous amount of energy required to fuel all of this growth results in big changes in eating and sleep patterns. Teenage boys continue to have high caloric requirements throughout the teen years; whereas, teenage girls experience a slowdown in physical growth, typically, during the early teen years.

Sleep Deprived Risk Takers

Teens need much more sleep than adults. They are not lazy. They are exhausted by the physical demands of growth. This exhaustion is worsened when teens do not get the 9-10 hours of sleep recommended for this stage of life.

Teens are also infamous for being risk takers. Risk taking is revved up during the teen years because the amygdala portion of the brain is "on fire". The amygdala is an important part of the "radar system" that generates the fight, flight and freeze survival response in all human brains.

The hyper vigilant activity of the amygdala along with the extreme hormonal changes explains the significant mood swings that are common during the teenage years. When parents are aware of the pressures that arise from these biological stresses, it becomes easier to understand how challenged teens feel. When parents also consider the social, cognitive and emotional demands to "fit in"; be self-aware; and successfully compete in school/sports/life that are placed on teens, it becomes even easier to understand how very challenging this period of human development truly is.

The Major Developmental Task of Teens

In the midst of all these rapid and extensive changes, the *major overall agenda during this period continues to be "identity formation"*. This is the toughest challenge of all. This means getting a sense of who one is in terms of values, disposition, behaviors, personality and so forth. It is no small task.

It is a time when children start to separate and further differentiate themselves from parents. It is a time when children seek greater approval and guidance from people other than parents. They especially look to their peers. It is the stage for that preps the "launch" into the adult portion of the life journey. Will it prepare for continued growth and wisdom? Or will it prep the child for a journey that is stymied by close mindedness; shame and fear; as well as anxiety and depression?

Keep Communication Channels Open

It is very important to note that when parents maintain safe and open channels of communication, children are better able to share difficult feelings and concerns. This means peers will assert less negative influence on them. The reason is simply that the parental value system has been and continues to be instilled through this open communication channel. Ultimately, it is important to remember that children want to stay in right relationship with parents; even as they struggle to figure out their own identity.

When the parenting principles of this course have been used during the magical thinking years of child development, a good foundation for open communication, active listening to feelings, emotional safety, trust, personal accountability, tolerance for distress and mutual respect will reduce and ideally prevent the power struggle dynamics that lead to oppositional teen behaviors. This means that despite the built-in challenges that normally accompany the teenage developmental period, teenagers will not act in the extreme manner depicted by the rebellious teen stereotype.

Even in this Stage...Power Struggle Dynamics Can be Extinguished or Reduced

If, on the other hand, your experience as a parent has been one of living through one power struggle after another, you still must know that it is not too late to change. Of course, years of entrenched habits are harder to overcome and so the challenge to make effective change is likely to be greater. Yet, it is important for you to know that these challenges have been met and overcome by other parents who commit to utilizing more effective communication skills and commit to modeling better coping skills.

The challenges with difficult or oppositional teens can still can be met and turned around. This means it is even more important for parents to change dysfunctional and ineffective patterns of listening and interacting as quickly as possible. The reality is that it will require more persistence to realize changes because of the enduring behavior patterns in both children and parents. It is important to remember that persistence is important; as is the willingness to model flexibility, the willingness to admit mistakes and the willingness to make repairs (more on this later).

Emotional Connections Matter

For now, it is important to remember that all people need emotional connections. Everyone, yes, everyone; even oppositional teens need good emotional connections. Healthy emotional connections allow people to feel loved and important. This is especially true for children, because they do not yet have the physical, cognitive, and emotional capabilities of adults.

Children are still developing in their capacities to discriminate the differences between what is vital to hear and what is vital to ignore. This means that a condemning or critical voice (from inside or outside one's head) has greater power to injure a child than an adult.

Strong emotional connections help create safe relationships for children so they can seek and get feedback. This will help them make better sense of the world. The capacity to experience one's authentic self in an emotionally close and safe relationship is a strong defense against experiencing anxiety and depression.

Children of all ages are Vulnerable

Children are truly *dependent* on the benevolence of their adult caregivers. This means they will develop whatever good or bad behaviors are felt necessary to get attention from parents; as this assures their survival (i.e. get their physical, cognitive and emotional needs met). This is why inconsistent parenting that is not sensitive to the real developmental capabilities of children makes it so very easy to accidentally train children to misbehave or seek the opinions of someone who will give them attention.

This is true throughout child development and can be especially problematic during the teen years.

Once again, the very good news is that all teens, even difficult and oppositional ones, will benefit from parents who learn and use the anxiety-busting communication and coping skills presented later in this workbook.

Workbook Exercise – Teenage Years

What key psychological developments occur during the teenage years?

_____

_____

_____

What physical and emotional challenges to teens face?

_____

_____

_____

T or F

Teens are naturally difficult and oppositional.

Teens are typically "lazy".

Teens are inclined to choose more risky behaviors than adults.

Teens will not try to separate and differentiate from parents who try to be their "friend" since all children are dependent upon parents.

Teens with emotionally health relationships with parents will not seek advice from negative peers.

Young Adults

Humans do not have fully developed adult brains until around 25 years of age. The changes in development may be more subtle during this last period of growth as it primarily involves the development of autonomy and emotional complexity. One of the most significant changes is that the stress hormone levels that were continuously rising throughout the teen years, finally peak at around age 22 and begin to taper down.

Once a child becomes an adult, the nature of the parent-child relationship can be one of friendship; based on love, trust and respect. Of course, parents will continue to have a leadership role to play, but as children become more competent adults, these roles are likely to shuffle around from time to time.

Workbook Exercise – Young Adults

What are two developments differentiate an adult brain from a teenage brain?

_____

_____

_____

_____

_____

_____

Communication Basics

There are very many reasons to become effective communicators. It almost goes without saying that great communicators are better prepared to tackle problems and are better at information sharing. As important as these reasons are for learning strong communication skills, they are just a subset of the most important reason for communicating well. The most important reason for communicating well is that it facilitates *emotional bonding*.

The Enormous Value in Communicating Effectively

Strong, well-rounded communicators facilitate a number of socially important things. They help people feel heard, feel important and to feel connected. When people communicate effectively, experiences of emotional isolation and emotional reactivity decrease. When this happens people feel more secure and understood. Emotional bonding leads to reductions in experiences of anxiety and depression.

Effective communicators are more open and willing to problem-solve in less rigid ways. This results in more effective problem-solving. People who are strong communicators are more effective in accessing, identifying and sharing their wants, needs and feelings. They become more willing to consider new perspectives and more inclined to drop maladaptive defenses which lead to emotional isolation.

The magic of this does not end here. Effective communication can yield these kind of results *even when people do not agree*. This is a very important point; it is not necessary to agree to achieve closeness, to feel respected, to feel heard, and to feel valued. It is necessary, however, to recognize the obstacles that block effective communication.

Obstacles to Effective Communication

There are four inadvertent but powerful communication blockers that parents commonly use. These are "telling", "trying to fix", "needing to be right" and "dismissing feelings". Let's investigate how these types of communication accidentally cause breaches in communication. After exploring these main types, other communication blockers will be reviewed.

Telling

Unless a person is in a situation where instruction is expected to take place, it is safe to say that most people do not enjoy "being told". It creates a power differential where the teller is "right" and the one being told is "clueless". It sets the stage for the person, who is being told, to feel a whole range of things. These include but are not limited to feeling: "stupid", "less than", "embarrassed", "resentful" and so forth.

Instructional Settings

"Telling" is usually most appropriate when used in instructional type situations. It may also be appropriate to "tell" someone what they should or should not do in some non-instructional situations. Safety situations, in particular, may warrant some immediate "telling". However, unless there is an emergency or some other urgency, "telling" has serious downsides. "Telling" creates those unpleasant power differentials previously mentioned and therefore, is a prime ingredient in creating and perpetuating power struggles.

Telling Pitfalls

Parents need to know that continued use of power struggles leads to oppositional youth behaviors. "Telling" also cuts the teller out of knowing what the intended listener's true perspective, dilemma or concern is. The teller may be making many boundary crossings (more on this later) which can generate anger in the listener. Ultimately, this impairs the listener's ability to truly hear the message the teller wishes to convey.

If you are like many parents, you may now be wondering, how you are to guide your child if you are not to "tell them" things. You may be wondering if your authority as a parent has been made null and void. You may be wondering how limits get set and whether your child will now "rule". *It is important for you to realize that you can put these fears aside.* When you use effective communication skills instead of inappropriate "telling", you will find that *your authority will be much greater and more respected* (more on this in the next section).

Trying to Fix

When children of all ages have problems to be solved, it is common for parents to rush in under the auspices of helping children to solve their problems. However, the most common outcome is that parents end up doing more *"rescuing"* than helping. Rescuing children, rather than guiding and truly helping, (more on this later) gives a bevy of accidental messages to children. These include but are not limited to: inadvertently conveying that the child is incapable of solving the problem (since it must be fixed in the way the parent suggests).

Accidental Messages

In addition to inadvertently conveying that the child needs "rescuing", other accidental messages may be given by the parent who tries to "fix". One such message is that the child's concern or feelings are not to be or can't be tolerated by the parent.

This especially happens when parents see their children emoting negative feelings. Many parents have a very low tolerance for seeing their children express negative emotions. As a result of this low tolerance, many parents react to "fix" the problem in order to remove the source of distress for themselves. Some parents just want to make their children "happy". Such parents need to realize that no one has the power or responsibility for "making" another person feel anything. This is because emotions are natural and specific to an individual (see Appendix F for the difference between core emotions and maladaptive defenses).

Other parents may just want the "complaining to stop". These parents not only give the message that emotions are "not okay" but that emotions are one and the same as behaviors (which they are not).

Boosting Problem-Solving Skills

The reality is, that even when parents have the very best intentions, the act of trying to "fix" someone else feels demeaning. It carries the accidental message that "I can and you cannot" figure this out.

Of course, in the case of children, it may very well be that they do not have the experience, maturity or information to be able to figure out their dilemmas. Parents still need to refrain from overt telling, because it is far better to actively involve children in dialogs that will help them develop problem-solving skills than it is to take the telling "short-cut".

Additionally, when parents jump into "fixing mode", they are also in danger of "fixing the wrong problem" since they have not taken the time to actively listen to their children's perspective and understand the problem as it appears to the child.

Needing to Be Right

Parents who need to be right in order to retain auras of authority or respect are actually inviting power struggle dynamics. This is because being "right" inevitably means the other person is "wrong" (or in a "one down position"). These parents also are inadvertently modeling a number of very negative coping and problem-solving actions. These negative coping and problem-solving skills include but are not limited to:

- Being inflexible

- Being close-minded and not being able to learn and assimilate/accommodate new information

- All or nothing thinking

- Inability to compartmentalize and break problems down into more specific and workable tasks

- Not modeling confidence about learning new information if one is in fact wrong.

Parents who seek to be right are demonstrating their need to appear perfect. Such a standard is unrealistic and sets a person up for so many problems including: limiting a person's willingness to try due to *fear of failure.*

Parents who need to be right are also less approachable. Children will be less inclined to seek the advice or support from a "know-it-all" parent and thus be more likely to seek the advice and/or consolation from a peer. A peer to your child may be less equipped than your child is to problem-solve. Even if the child is more equipped than your child is to problem-solve, the peer will be less equipped than a competent adult. Additionally, the peer is not from your child's family and so is likely to have a value system that is different from your family.

Overall, parents who invest in being "right", risk alienating their children. It leaves children feeling alone, misunderstood and vulnerable to being misguided by negative peers or those who may be even more clueless as to how to best solve the problems at hand.

Dismissing Feelings

Parents need to remember that they become effective leaders when they focus on setting limits around *problem behaviors rather than setting limits around negative emotions*. When parents try to limit the expression of negative emotions, they risk: alienating their children; setting up power struggles and inadvertently training their children to "stuff" or "deny" their own feelings.

When children's feelings are dismissed by parents, the children learn that it is "not okay" to feel such a way. They learn to view such feelings as "dangerous" and that these feelings jeopardize their relationship with their caregivers. This is a scary experience for children of all ages. The end result is that children learn to block, deny or suppress feelings; even to the point that they become out-of-touch with their core emotions. Not being in touch with feelings, not being knowledgeable about how to cope with feelings and not knowing how to effectively address the problems that the core emotions are signaling contributes to the development of anxiety and depression in childhood and also in adult years (see Appendix F on Core Emotions).

Workbook Exercise – Communication Blockers

Name and describe four communication blockers that impair parenting.

_____

_____

_____

What inadvertent messages are given when parents inappropriately use "telling" and "trying to fix" styles of communication?

_____

_____

_____

_____

_____

_____

What problems arise from perfectionism and parents who need to be "right"?

_____

_____

_____

Other Communication Blockers

The following communication blockers should be eliminated from exchanges with children and other adults as well.

Labeling and name calling – this feels demeaning to a person, magnifies one aspect of the person and diminishes other important qualities. Labels have a tendency to "stick" and color the way a person sees oneself later on in life.

Judging – this promotes power struggles since the judged person is likely to counter the negative assessment received. Whether the child objects or not, judgments feel painful and can lead the child to rebel, isolate or suffer silently.

All or nothing assessments – this models rigid and catastrophic thinking to children. It is not only unsettling to a child, it also reduces the ability to consider alternatives that can actually lead to effective problem-solving. It sends the messages that problems are overwhelming rather than things to be addressed and solved. Modeling this type of thinking to children _helps teaches them to be more fearful, rigid and less willing to take risks to grow._

Fearful people are more inclined to externalize (blame others; blame the world) and this is a very helpless victim-like stance to take. People who use all or nothing thinking, catastrophize, are rigid and poor problem-solvers, and blame others are creating behavior patterns that lead right to the heart of anxiety and depression syndromes. It is important to remember that it is not possible to change as long as one views oneself as a "victim" since by definition, victims are helpless. Life is full of both problems and risks and it is very handicapping to use this type of communication with people of all ages; especially children.

Blame – this leads to people feeling wounded and encourages defensive behaviors which aid the further deterioration of communication. Blame-style communication does not contribute to feeling emotionally connected; rather it contributes to feelings of resentment. It also contributes to feeling that one is "less than", "defective" and/or a "victim" (see "All or Nothing" section above).

Sarcasm and ridicule – this is a biting form of defense used by a person who seeks to communicate a "one up position". Sarcasm is a verbal attack which leaves the receiver of the sarcastic sound bite in a "one down" position. Thus sarcasm contributes to power struggles and feelings of being "less than". The sarcastic person may feel "witty" (a "one up position") but it is at the expense of the other person. It also reminds children of their "inferior" status, since they are not typically "privileged" to be sarcastic back to parents.

"You" statements (as in "you do this", "you do that" often combined with "always" or "never" or other all or nothing assessments) – these comments feel accusatory to the receiver of them and thus promote defensiveness.

Yelling and overreacting – the person who is yelling tries to overpower the other person by the loud and profuse volume of their words; however, rather than demonstrating power, the yeller is signaling loss of control. It is not by accident that we say that a yelling person has "lost it" or is "overwhelmed". Yellers are essentially telling the world "this is the best I can do to cope" and that their abilities to emotionally regulate and respond are gone. It also creates a double standard, in that, parents are allowed to do it but the children are not. It is not an effective behavior to model to children.

Shutting down and denial – these are avoidant defenses and give the message to children that they or their problems are not important or are too troublesome to address. Parents can set and defend healthy boundaries instead (more on this later).

Over-explaining- messages to children need to be succinct and age-appropriate. As mentioned earlier, when parents over-explain, they accidentally elevate children to adult status and invite children to negotiate or debate. This is unfair to children, since they will not have adult brains until the age of 25. This means that children do not have the capacity to think as adults.

When disciplining children, it is very important not to over-explain as a response to behavioral infractions. At such times it is important to simply deliver age-appropriate and predefined consequences. Parents need to remember that children should only be disciplined for misbehaviors and not for the feelings that underlie them (limits and consequences need to be decided and agreed upon in advance; more on this later).

Over-explaining during time of consequence delivery invites debate. It leads children to label unrelenting parents as "unfair". Children who do successfully negotiate against a parent's explanations will develop feelings of entitlement; this will encourage future debates.

Mind Reading – this occurs when people believe they can derive and interpret other people's feelings and thoughts from their facial expressions, statements or actions. Certainly, the probability of an accurate "read" goes up when a person knows another person very well. The probability of an accurate "read" also goes up when the "reader" is keenly paying attention to the things that are said and done. However, it still remains a "best guess" since no one can know for certain what is in another person's mind. This margin of doubt fuels power struggles.

It is also not possible to accurately judge a person's motives. Such assessments are likely to be largely colored by the mind reader's point of view. This also contributes to power struggle dynamics; even when "read" very accurately. The child relies on the margin of doubt that will always exist and so can default to the reasonable premise that the contents of one's mind is private and can stay private.

Most people feel indignant and misunderstood when another claims to know what another person's motives are. Parents need to carefully "pick their battles" and mind reading is one battle that they are never going to "win". Besides, having a winner and loser is a sure sign that power struggles are in play. Mind reading is full of so many faulty assumptions. These lead to misunderstandings and resentment.

Workbook Exercise – Other Communication Blockers

Name and describe at least 3 other communication blockers.

_____

_____

_____

List and discuss 5 communication blockers that contribute to anxiety and depression patterns of thinking and behaving.

_____

_____

_____

_____

_____

_____

What types of communication patterns are easy to recognize? Which ones are harder to detect?

_____

_____

_____

Effective Communication – What You Need to Do

"I" messages

"I" messages are very effective because they allow you to convey what you think and feel in a non-judgmental fashion. They provide your perspective and are not perceived by others as threatening (as are "you" messages which feel attacking). "I" messages may feel unnatural and even silly to the person who is not used to using them. Despite this initial awkward period, "I" messages remain a very effective communication tool to use. "I" messages can be used to avoid mind reading and the perception of attack that "you" messages give. Rather than making assumptions, it is far better to simply state your concern or feeling; e.g. "I am worried that x will happen"; "I am concerned that you think x" and so forth. "I" messages help to prevent power struggles.

Allows for Authenticity

Very importantly, "I" messages allow a person to assert what is true for that person and assert it in a way that cannot be disputed. For example, "I am angry about the mess that has not been cleaned". No one could reasonably respond "you are not angry" because the "I" message speaker would simply respond "I am". No one can dispute the way you legitimately feel. The "I" message person is not assigning blame and is likely to be making a statement of authentic feeling.

If the listener is in doubt about what the "I" message person is conveying, a better respond would be, "Oh, it seems like you are not angry" or "it sounds like you are furious". Statements that use "seems like", "sounds like", "I wonder what that is like" and so forth are safe ways to further the discussion initiated by the "I" message speaker. This is because such statements honor what the person has said and invite further clarification (see the next section on "Active Listening").

"I" messages still might be threatening to a defensive person who has an inability to tolerate the negative emotions expressed by another person. The only necessary defense of an "I" statement that is challenged by such a defensive person is to simply reaffirm it with an appropriate "I am" or "I do" (otherwise debates and dismissal are likely to follow).

Workbook Exercise – "I" Messages

Describe the importance of using "I" messages.

_____
_____
_____
_____
_____
_____

Do people need to justify their feelings? What is a good way for a person to respond when someone questions the feelings a person stated?

_____
_____
_____
_____
_____
_____

Active listening

Active listening is a skill that needs to be developed and practiced. As the name correctly implies, it involves deliberate action. It does not occur when a listener just passively hears the words another says. Active listening means paying close attention, not only to the content being said, but more importantly, to the feelings that seem to be conveyed along with the content.

Active Listening Involves Actions

Active listening involves "checking in" with the person who is speaking. This demonstrates to the speaker that the listener is paying attention and also helps to eliminate any faulty impressions. A good way to "check in" is to make "seems like" or "sounds like" statements (e.g. "Seems like you are angry" or "Sounds like you are really worried about it" or "Seems like you had a bad day"). Notice that the goal of the listener is to try to identify and empathize with the feelings of the speaker. The goal is not try to "fix" the speaker's problem(s). Problem-solving is more likely to naturally evolve out of the conversation after feelings are accessed and identified. When this happens, parents can actively guide children through the process of problem-solving (more on this later).

Listening does not necessarily mean agreeing...It means Mapping

It is important to note that the listener does not have to be in agreement as to "why" the person is feeling what they feel. The goal is to listen to what the other person is experiencing and to help them "map" it. Mapping emotions (also addressed in the Child Development section) is the way children learn to understand and make use of their feelings. Without getting feedback from a loving adult, children do not know what the uncomfortable sensations of negative emotions signal. When parents "check in" with "seems like...." Or "sounds like...." they are helping children identify a word that describes what they feel; hence, they are helping children to make sense of it; they are "mapping" it.

Social Regulation through Mapping

There are very many studies from the field of neuroscience that support the concept of social regulation through "mapping" (Siegel, 2010). The studies (Booth & Jernberg, 2010; Greenberg & Watson, 2005) show that active listening to feelings is extremely important tool for helping others map and regulate highly charged emotions. When parents help "map" the child's emotional experience, they are helping children to access, identify and process the energy portion of their emotions. "Processing" the energy component of emotions helps to take the charge out of the emotion. When a child feels understood and an appropriate descriptive word is assigned to the feeling, the rational centers of the brain are better able to engage in problem-solving (see below section on self-regulation also see Appendix F for more on Core Emotions).

Additionally, emotional isolation is reduced when feelings are "mapped". This is due to people feeling connected when others "get" how they feel. Attunement (Van der Kolk, 2014) is critical for developing emotional intimacy and overcoming the rifts created by experiences of trauma.

In general, when people use active listening to acknowledge the feelings of another person, that person is helped to access and identify what is being experienced and this helps calm the person to calm down. This is a very important skill for parents to have since "social regulation" helps children learn the skill of emotionally regulating themselves.

Self-regulation evolves from Social Regulation Mapping

Teaching a child to be effective in emotional self-regulation is one of the most important tasks that parents need to accomplish. Here is why: children who effectively self-regulate are better problem-solvers; are more capable of developing emotional intimacy; and have less incidence of anxiety, depression, addictions, and oppositional defiance. In general, it is safe to say that children who learn how to regulate their emotions will use and develop better coping skills; be able to be more attentive and consequently do better in school. They will have better skills for leading more balanced lives; even though challenges come.

Self-regulation skills evolves from social regulation. As a parent attempts to help a child socially regulate, the parent helps the child learn important skills which the child will duplicate when attempting to self-regulate. This process requires helping the child become adept at identifying feelings. In order to do this, the parent, who is listening, needs to be paying close attention and needs to communicate (once again "map" not "tell") their experience of what the child appears to be feeling.

Active Listening Utilizes Many Skills

When "mapping" another person's feelings, (Siegel, 2010), it is important to avoid being a "mind reader" or using any of the other negative listening traps (see previous section on ineffective communication methods). A person who "maps" feelings, invites the speaker to affirm or negate whether the "seems like" or "sounds like" is an accurate assessment.

Even when the emotionally charged person disagrees with the listener's assessment as to what the feeling is, the social regulation process is still happening. This is because the emotionally charged speaker can begin to reflect, assess and identify what he or she is actually feeling (e.g. "No, I am not angry....I am just frustrated" etc.). When a person identifies an emotion...whether it be recognizing one's own emotion (self-regulation) or helping someone else to identify an emotion (social regulation), the emotional "charge" is lessened.

Identifying emotions with words moves them from the non-verbal portions of the brain to the executive portions of the brain. This is where the verbal, logical and problem solving centers of the brain exist. So as you may have already realized, it is not until an emotion is identified with a word that the brain can begin to effectively problem-solve.

This is why it does not make any sense *to reason* with a person who is emotionally charged and acting out. It is a much more effective path to help people calm down through actively listening and help them identify the feelings being experienced. It is a matter of exploring descriptions and words to find what resonates with the feeling being expressed. This helps the symbolic, non-verbal language of the emotional right brain take a more "concrete shape" that both the listener and emotionally active person can now share through spoken language. This shared experience also helps move abstract thoughts from the symbolic emotive centers of the brain to the logical, serial processing centers of the brain; thus problem-solving becomes more possible.

Undivided Attention

People soon recognize that it is not possible to be doing or focusing on something else while trying to actively listen. When your children are trying to tell you something that is important to them and you are cooking, cleaning, or doing something else that distracts you, the amount of attention you will be giving to what they say will be compromised. Children will recognize that you are not fully present and this feels dismissive and hurtful (no matter how legitimately busy you are). It is far better to tell a child, "It sounds like what you have to tell me is important and I really want to hear it. Right now, I cannot give you the attention to hear you the way that I want. Let's talk about this when I am not distracted cooking, driving etc. "(or....depending on the circumstances.... "Let's talk about it when I can wind down from work in a half hour").

Active Listening Benefits Everyone

Active listening benefits adults and children a like. Here is a very simple example to illustrate the value of being actively heard:

Let's pretend you are working as a bagger in the check-out area of a very busy grocery store and are struggling to sort groceries into the bags. You want the bags to be easy to carry and you want to bag in a timely manner. As the line begins to get longer and customers become more overtly annoyed at you, you turn to the cashier for emotional support. Much to your dismay, you see that the cashier's attitude has joined that of the disgruntled customers. Soon, there are even more customers making rude remarks to you. The attitudes and actions of these people are very stressful to you and soon begin to overwhelm your capacity to stay focused on the job. You really feel a need to go home and tell someone who cares about you all about your stressful day.

When you arrive at home and talk to the important person in your life, which response would you like to hear?

   a. Well....they really are right you know....you are a terrible bagger....you always put too many cans in one bag. I can teach you how to bag better.

   b. Oh my...sounds like you had a really bad day. What happened?

Hopefully, it is obvious that answer B is the more emotionally supportive answer. Yet, if it is so obvious, what do you suppose is happening when so many people actually respond to distressed children, family and spouses with some version of answer A?

When people dive in to "fix" the problem (as the person in answer "A" attempts to do), they are in essence trying to relieve the distress they experience when they hear of the other person's negative thoughts, feelings and situation. They do not want or like that the other person is unhappy, stressed, overwhelmed and so forth. They want to "make it better" and so they jump in with advice to remedy the perceived problem as quickly as possible.

As you may now gather, "jumping in with a solution" is generally not appreciated or welcomed by the distress person who really just wants to be understood. When a person provides a solution in a very short period (sometimes in a matter of seconds), the distressed person is likely to react in a less than receptive way. It is as if "salt" has been added to their "wounds". They may be thinking, "You must think that I am stupid, since you can instantly solve a problem that I could not solve all day". Now instead of feeling understood, there is an even greater sense of being alone. The person, who wants support, is likely to react to your attempts to "fix" him/her by becoming snappish or irrational. If the "fixer" gets defensive, the stage is being further set for an argument to develop. This is not what the stressed person hoped to receive upon coming home.

Nuts and Bolts of Active Listening

So what then does active listening do? Does it mean that you have to agree with a stressed person just to appease him/her? The answer to the first question is that active listening helps a person regulate feelings, and helps calm a person so as to be better positioned for problem-solving. The answer to the second question is no. You can actively listen to a distressed person, hear feelings and not even agree with anything being said.

After all, there is no right or wrong when it comes to emotions (do not confuse emotions with behaviors). People simply feel what they feel. Negative feelings are activated when a person's "radar system" is triggered by something in the environment that presents as a threat. The non-verbal centers of the brain are alerted (this includes the amygdala portion of the brain mentioned in the teen years section). When the risk is assessed to be significant, fight/flight/freeze modes are triggered. The "threat" can be an actual danger in the environment or it can be a perceived threat that stems from the way the neural pattern was "wired" during childhood (i.e. during a time when the immature brain of a child adaptively responded to feel safe).

A Whole lot of Neuroscience Involved

The "radar system" includes the amygdala, brain stem and other non-verbal centers of the brain which have been "wired" to interpret a triggering event in a particular way. Thus, there does not need to be a "good" or "valid" reason to be angry, sad, and afraid since this type of reasoning is not located in the amygdala and adjacent areas. Reasoning is located in the pre-frontal cortex portion of the brain.

Though this has previously been stated, it is important enough to repeat. In order to move the amygdala generated signal from the non-verbal portion of the brain to the logical, verbal center of the brain, *people need to actively label the feeling with a word.*

Feelings Detective

When distressed people are unable to label the feeling, it is important to help them play detective. The "detective work" begins by investigating the way the distress is experienced the in the body. The very act of noticing things such as a "rapid heart beat", "queasy stomach", "headache", "foggy thinking", "blurred vision", "jelly legs", just to name a few common anxiety symptoms, will help a person calm down. This happens because when people notice something in the body, the executive portion of the brain sends a message to the "radar system". This executive center message signals to the lower regions of the brain that the "distress message has been received". The feeling/radar system has now served its purpose; i.e. it flagged the problem that needs to be solved and the executive branch "gets it".

Calming Down Generates Better Problem-Solving

When an active listener takes the time to actually hear a distressed person and help that person identify the specifics of a concern, the activation energy portion of the emotion is reduced. Hence, the person is not so "emotionally charged" because the call to action has been heeded. Thus the active listener helps the distressed person calm down and this facilitates moving toward problem-solving.

Honing in, on the particular aspects of a feeling such as anger, aids in identifying the type, size and scope of the problem. For example, angry feelings indicate problems involving a boundary crossing of some sort (see Appendix F for further information on Core Emotions). Active listening comments such as "sounds like you are angry" allow upset people to reflect on what seems to ring true about their experiences; e.g. "No, I am actually, embarrassed". This leads people to figure out what they want to do about the actual problem (e.g. "I am embarrassed" or "I feel stupid") rather than the initial presenting problem (e.g. "I cannot bag groceries").

Questions to Guide and Build Problem-Solving Skill

Once a person has calmed down and is able to identify the real issue underlying the distress, the active listener can further help the problem-solving process by asking "what" and "how" questions. These type of questions further honor the person since the person still feels heard, supported and respected as a person who is capable of solving problems. This is done when the active listener simply asks questions such as: "What do you want to do about it?"; "What would you like to see happen?" or "How would that work out?"

Empathy Reduces Emotional Isolation

In the example of the grocery bagger, if the person identified a negative feeling such as "embarrassed because they treat me as if I am stupid", an empathetic response would always be appropriate (e.g. "yeah that stinks"). The important thing to note is that you can say, "that stinks" with all sincerity because it does "stink" to feel embarrassed and feel as if people think you are stupid. Notice that you can empathize even if you do agree with the level of distress. In the case of the grocery bagger, you can even believe the person is an ineffective bagger. The active listener can then follow up by sincerely asking, "What would you like to see happen?"

Guide Children with Questions that help them Problem-Solve

As we continue the example of the distressed grocery bagger, the distressed person may present as somewhat calmer, after being actively heard and queried appropriately, however, the distressed person may still be largely generating emotive answers; e.g. "I want to quit my job". This type of response from children will frequently trigger a parental launch into the "telling mode". This is likely due to the parent's amygdala now sending out a fear message (e.g. "my child is a quitter" or "my child won't have another job for the whole summer and will just be hanging around" and so forth).

A much better response than launching into "telling mode" is to invite the child (or any distressed person) into problem-solving by simply asking "What would happen if you did do that?" (E.g. quit your job). Another appropriate response might be, "I wonder how that would work out for you?"

These responses are very powerful because they fit in with the way the human brain works. Whenever people hear questions (whether if is from someone speaking to them or they hear it on the radio, or overhear another conversation), human brains fill in the blank after a question. Our brains do not like uncertainty and unanswered questions. So human brains provide the answers. This is a very natural process. Even when people shrug their shoulders and refuse to give an answer, the probability is extraordinarily high that they have answered it in their minds. The only reason a person might not have "answered" it would be if they genuinely do not know; however, even then, the person is answering the question by thinking "I don't know".

Children Benefit from Learning How to Reach Their Own Solutions

Problem-solving is much more effective when people are able to come to their own conclusions. People who arrive at their own conclusion of "I do not know" are more likely to wonder what can be done than people who feel shame or anger about being told what to do. Shame or anger just re-starts the firing of alert signals in the amygdala. This confuses things by adding more problems before the original one has been solved.

When a distressed person has nothing further to add, appears stumped or says "I don't know" then it is still appropriate and best to ask another question. Questions such as "Would you like to hear my thoughts?" or statements such as "I wonder if you would like to have me help you figure this out" are useful. Using an "I wonder" type of statement is as powerful as asking "what" and "how" questions, because when people say they are wondering about something, we wonder along with them (even if we do not muse about it out loud).

Parents need to be satisfied with knowing that even when their children present as stubborn and unwilling to participate in problem-resolution, the "what" and "how" questions and the "I wonder" statements are helping them think about the issues. Parents need to know that this is true, even if it occurs privately inside their children's minds. Since asking "how" and "what" questions and making "I wonder" statements are so very thought provoking, they are very important communication tools parents can use to help children develop critical thinking. These questions and statement prompt children to think about how the problem can be solved (including what might and might not work).

Do not ask "Why"

Notice that it is important not to be asking "why" questions; as these questions attempt to elicit reasons. Reasons require logical thinking from the executive centers of the brain. It is important to remember that when people are receiving strong emotional signals that they are reacting from the non-verbal, symbolic (non-logical) portions of the brain. "Why" questions can be asked when a person is responding in a calm and logical way. However, it is still important to note that "why" questions elicit reasons and that if used inappropriately, parents can be inadvertently inviting power struggles since children will attempt to negotiate with their reasons. Asking "why" too early in the problem-solving cycle also will elicit "excuses" rather than uncovering the real source of the emotional distress (i.e. the real problem). Because of this, it is a more effective plan to guide children with "what"/"how" and "I wonder" questions and statements.

Problem-solving and Increased Closeness

A parent with strong active listening skills is able to guide children very effectively by just asking the appropriate questions and making the appropriate statements. Additionally, children will feel heard and not dismissed (since parents, who practice active listening, refrain from "telling"); they will remain in good relationship with parents (and are likely to feel closer to parents); will be less likely to resort to oppositional behavior; will learn to calm themselves; will take themselves seriously and feel empowered (because as a parent you are modeling that you do take their thoughts and feelings seriously; even when they need further guidance, information and clarification) and so will become confident, competent and flexible people.

Those last three qualities are essential for good mental health and are antidotes to anxiety and depression. Mental health will prevail even when children are faced with difficult life challenges when they develop solid life skills. When parents develop the parenting skills outlined in this workbook, they will help children build those life skills.

Active Listening Summary

Children who are actively heard by their parents will feel validated as people instead of feeling dismissed and helpless (people who feel helpless view themselves as ineffective; this is a key ingredient that fuels anxiety) (Yapko, 2009). It is essential for parents to recognize that validating children's thoughts, feelings and opinions does not mean that you need to agree with them. Active listening does not mean that you forget about setting and enforcing limits. It simply means you hear what your child feels, consider what it means to your child, and are fully present to have a meaningful dialog about it. By doing this is a loving way, relationships ruptures will not occur since you will be viewed as a much sought after safe harbor. As such, your children will seek you when they are troubled instead of negative peers or other uninformed if well-meaning persons. This means you will remain an important resource for children; even when they become adults.

Workbook Exercise – Active Listening

Describe active listening.

_____

_____

_____

Describe the importance of active listening.

_____

_____

_____

Describe some possible negative consequences that result from not actively listening.

_____

_____

_____

Healthy Boundaries

Parents need to help children recognize, set and defend healthy boundaries for themselves and recognize and respect the boundaries set by other people. The skill of healthy boundary setting and defense will help your child more effectively fend off negative peer pressure (note parents can develop skill in healthy boundaries by listening to the auditory component of this workbook; see Appendix A). Healthy boundary building skills also help children develop greater self-awareness. This is because boundary setting requires having knowledge of one's values in order to know what boundary to make and where to set it.

This skill needs to be especially strong during the teen years when children are focusing on identity formation and figuratively, "chomping at the bit" to break away from parents. Because of these issues, teens may be more vulnerable to peer pressure than are children in other age groups; that is, of course, unless they have been helped to create and defend strong boundaries.

What is a healthy personal boundary?

A boundary is a limit that one sets around oneself (Cloud & Townsend, 1992). A boundary helps define oneself and it tells the world what a person values, believes, likes, and dislikes. It tells the world how much a person will "take" or "not take" when others attempt to "walk over" him or her.

Boundaries Require Self-Awareness

When people are aware of their boundaries, they are more apt to take action to uphold them than when they are uncertain about "what they will take or not take". When children are uncertain about boundaries, they are left to sort things out "on the fly" rather than taking action to defend what they already know about themselves; e.g. when a child knows "I don't cheat", the thinking "I will not let someone look over my shoulder during the test" will be more readily accessible. When children do not know where they need to place boundaries, they remain a mystery to themselves as well as others since they are not telling themselves or others "where they stand".

Family Values make Good Boundaries

Parents have a key role to play in helping children learn how, when and where to set and defend boundaries. When parents guide through "what" and "how" questions as well as through "I wonder" statements, they create a safe place for children to begin exploring family values and what it means to be a person who lives by values. Parents need to allow children to have a voice to say "no"; otherwise, they cannot be expected to know how to say "no" when they really need to say it. When children have poor boundaries, they will be less alert to when other people make socially inappropriate boundary crossings and will tend to miss "red flags" when forming relationships (a red flag is a signal that the behavior of another person warrants further investigation to more fully understand the size, scope and current danger of the "red flag" person's potentially problematic behavior).

Bullies and Boundaries

Since people use boundaries to alert the world as to "what they will take and what they won't take", people with weak boundaries are flagging to bullies and other controlling types of people that they won't resist when boundaries are crossed. People with weak boundaries, of course, do not intend to send "I won't resist" messages, but that is what they do and this is why some people seem to get picked on more than other people. It is also why some people seem to continuously find one abusive romantic partner after another (even after just leaving one). The failure to set and defend healthy boundaries is behind these type of concerns as is the need to discern where other people set and defend boundaries.

Workbook Exercise – Healthy Personal Boundary

Describe what a healthy personal boundary is.

_____
_____
_____

Describe your understanding of a "red flag". What seems to be important about recognizing "red flags"?

_____
_____
_____

How to Set a Boundary

In order to set boundaries, people need to know what they value, believe, like and dislike. Parents can help children form a value system when they see parents act on and model the behaviors they say are important. It is not enough for parents to just tell children something; parents need to follow up words with actions. It is more than just a saying; actions do speak volumes louder than words. Parents who describe values and then act according to them are powerfully teaching their values to their children. So, for example, if you want your children to be good citizens who are able to regulate their temper in a socially appropriate way, it is not acceptable for parents to model anything that violates these values (e.g. not paying for something because it had not added to the check; yelling when one is upset; using curse words; drinking excessively; smoking and so forth). Parents also need to model taking actions to effectively defend boundaries in a pro-social way.

Pro-social Boundary Setting

Helping children to appropriately say "no" is an important first boundary defense skill. Children begin using this boundary setting skill when they first recognize their own personhood around the age of two. It is the time when they start defining what they like, want and "what they will take and not take".

Unfortunately, parents often do not recognize the significance of this "saying no" milestone; rather they, too often, see it as nothing more than a time of terrible obstinacy. While it is true that the two year old mind is very immature and by nature presents significant challenges to parents, it is important that parents do not inadvertently send the message that saying "no" is bad.

The Importance of Being Developmentally Appropriate

It is important for parents to note that working within the developmental capabilities of a child, rather than against them, makes parents' lives easier while also helping children to feel safe and attached. This is especially true whenever the world presents as scary and distressing. Developmentally appropriate parenting takes into consideration the maturity of the child's brain, sets appropriate limits and consequences and helps the child to regulate emotions. For example, in the case of a young child, parents can provide a couple of parent-approved choices so the child still feels a sense of personal power or parents can redirect a child to do something that is calming. Additionally parents can use calming tones and hugs. They can give advance warnings so as to help children make better transitions.

Active Listening to Help Build Boundaries

Parents should also use active listening skills to empathize with the child who is saying no; even when the parent needs to redirect a child and/or enforce a limit. The goal is always to help the child develop skills; rather than to control or defeat them. Parents can state this purpose to their children; e.g. "It seems that this is hard for you. I am sorry that it is. I am trying to help you learn this because it is important....even though it is hard". This helps your child retain dignity rather than feeling separated from you and shamed about saying "no". Active listening helps parents avoid participating in power struggle dynamics.

Parents as Role Models for Boundaries

Parents can model setting boundaries with the use of "I" statements. This happens when a parent creates a boundary by saying "That is something I do not do" or "I am not interested" or "that is not for me" (the last example is a variation of the "I" statement). Notice that the boundary is asserted with the simple statement as to what one will or will not do. There is no need for an explanation (unless the person would like to give a simple one when warranted). Giving unnecessary explanations tends to invite counter arguments which may lead to relaxing or relinquishing of the boundary.

When such a boundary is asserted, it can stand on its own. For example when a person says "that is not something I can do" and someone tries to counter it, the boundary defense just gets reiterated... "Sorry, I don't". Anyone who knows how to respect a boundary will stop insisting that you do something that you maintain you can't or won't.

Workbook Exercise – Setting a Healthy Boundary

Describe how to set a healthy boundary.

_____
_____
_____

Describe the importance of being able to say "no".

_____
_____
_____

Boundary Defense

Your children will encounter people who do not respect their boundaries. They will encounter subtle as well as blatant "walk all over you" boundary crossings. Parents will help their children enormously by teaching them how to defend their boundaries in a pro-social way. This means teaching children to keep their eyes on the real issue at hand (the boundary crossing) rather than reacting in a way that "muddies" the original problem. In muddied cases, the child who suffers the original boundary crossing becomes part of the problem. When this happens, it becomes hard for supervising adults to dispense justice.

In order for children to learn pro-social boundary defending skills, they need to practice a whole subset of other skills. These include: staying focused on the original problem (or goal to have the problem stopped or rectified); stopping impulses to act out and get revenge (includes impulse control, self-discipline, emotional regulation); and acting in a confident and assertive way. And so, you can see that healthy boundary defense is quite a complex life skill. It is not easy for children to learn because the skills are complex and boundary crossings can occur in so many less than obvious ways.

Children will benefit when helped by parents who are developmentally appropriate and utilize active listening skills. This will help children to feel heard (rather than having their concerns dismissed as trivial); to identify their feelings, to emotionally regulate and to become better problem-solvers.

In order for children to practice boundary defense, children need to also continue to develop awareness of "what they will or will not take" and "what is right and what is wrong". Children need to have parents who will help them sort out the confusion.

First Line of Defense

Once a boundary is established, the first line of defense for that boundary is the ability to say "no". Of course, in order to be able to do so, children need to have been taught that it is okay to say "no". This means children need to feel that their opinions count (even when an adult or peer disagrees); rather than having to be silently compliant or in fear of disapproval or punishment. Discomfort with being able to say "no" is possibly a contributor to the poor results of Nancy Reagan's "Just Say No to Drugs" campaign in the 1980s.

Stronger Statement and Warning about Impending Action

Even when children are successful in saying "no" and using "I" statements, there will still be plenty of times when their boundaries will continue to be pushed by inconsiderate, or clueless others who persist in pushing their own agendas. The second line of the defense then needs to kick it. This may be a use of stronger statements and perhaps a warning of an impending action; e.g. "I am getting frustrated because I do not feel heard", "I would like to change the topic", "I will not continue this conversation unless you stop yelling/insisting/cursing etc." "If you do not stop yelling,

I am going to leave the room/hang up the phone and we will need to continue when you are calmer etc." Of course, the type of statements made will depend on the age of the child and the situation.

Deliver the Action

After the stronger statements are made and a warning of impending action to support the boundary are given, children need to have the skill and confidence to turn the warning into action. Parents need to model the active defense of boundaries to children in daily family life.

Parents have lots of opportunities to model the setting and defending of boundaries; e.g. when they do not allow themselves to get "stretched too thin" by saying "yes" to too many things and by not being able to say "no"; when they take action to end a conversation whenever another person starts to yell, becomes abusive or becomes dysregulated. When another family member has become dysregulated and starts to yell, it is appropriate for the person who is defending boundaries (e.g. the boundary "I will be treated respectfully") to give a warning (e.g. "I will have to leave if we can not discuss this more calmly") and the ultimately leave or change the topic (whatever is an appropriate response and not a charged reaction). It may also be appropriate to tell the other person, "I am not rejecting you....I just won't participate in this type of conversation" and "We can resume the conversation when there is no yelling".

Repeat Boundary Offenders

If you or your children begin to recognize that certain people are blatant and repeat boundary crossing offenders, you will need to help your children come to the realization that this friendship/relationship may need to be kept at a more removed level or terminated if so warranted. Parents can help children process any sadness about the loss of it as well as any other feelings that arise as a result of the boundary crossing and defense of it.

Workbook Exercise – Defending Healthy Boundaries

Describe the sequence of how to defend a boundary.

_____

_____

_____

Describe how to help someone make a repair after crossing a boundary.

_____

_____

_____

Giving Unconditional Love while Being Strict

It is important to remember that being firm and being strict are not polar opposites to being loving and approachable. Being firm and strict simply means that you do what you say you will do (e.g. enforce limits in the manner you say you will). Even though children might prefer that you back off and become a "softy", it is never in their interest to do so. When parents position the things they say as "negotiable", parents are setting themselves up for debates; arguments; begging and pleading; and power struggle dynamics (as previously described: power struggles can be identified by whether someone "wins" and the other "loses"; although in reality, both parties lose because the relationship is compromised). Power struggle dynamics is a key ingredient in the creation of oppositional children (see section 7 on Appropriate and Realistic Expectations for Life for a further discussion of power struggles).

Challenges

Oppositional Children

Oppositional children do not know how to delay their impulses. If oppositional children are not gratified, they become so emotionally distraught that they become dysregulated. This means that they cannot deal with and cannot contain the emotional energy that accompanies their negative emotions. And so, they begin to act out. As is, too often, the case, dysregulated children may become quite volatile. Depending on the age and size of the child, the behaviors can be very destructive to properties and other people. When a child is acting in such a way, parents feel helpless and often seek to appease the child in any way; this includes giving in to the child's demands in some form or another. This is a huge error in judgment because it inadvertently trains the child that "temper tantrums work".

Parents need to be firm and loving even when faced with the difficult challenges of oppositional children. Even though oppositional children may present as callous and detached, they are simply using maladaptive defenses. In reality, they are feeling lost, confused and emotionally isolated. They very much need the guidance of a firm and unconditionally loving parent. Unconditional love is not the same thing as "anything goes".

Temper Tantrums

Temper tantrums are not something that people simply "out grow". Two year olds infamously throw themselves on the ground because their bodies are so flooded with the energy of negative emotions that they are not yet able to name or describe. Without guidance, the very best they can do is to act out via body throwing, hitting, screaming, crying, biting or any other method that helps them to discharge the flood of emotional energy. Such a child is already overwhelmed, so it has little benefit to scream at or bully the child into compliance. When parents yell at, threaten, or yank a dysregulated child, they are not only adding to the dysregulation but they are casting themselves as someone who is scary instead of comforting. When children are dysregulated, *they need a safe and in-charge parent* who will help them calm down. Helping children calm down, does not mean giving in or surrendering limits or skipping consequences. It means strictly enforcing the rules. It does not mean joining or avoiding the dysregulation at hand.

Strict and Loving – An Important Partnership

When children are oppositional or throwing temper tantrums, children are at a loss as to how to better manage the situations and themselves. Being dysregulated is a disturbing internal experience for children as well as a disturbing exterior experiences for parents and others. Because it is very important for children to stay in relationship with their caregivers and to not experience shame (as this furthers dysregulation and harms self-esteem), it is very important for parents to respond with unconditional love; even when having to strictly enforce the rules and impose strong limits.

No License to Act Out; No license to Abuse

This is how a parent helps a child to socially regulate and ultimately self-regulate. These are complex life skills that will continue to be developed just as good boundary defense skills need to be constantly tweaked. No matter what situations children experience, they need to learn how to regulate themselves; and whether they are angry, disappointed, frustrated, sad, and fearful and so on, they need to learn that strong and unpleasant emotions do not give them license to behaviorally act out.

Parents need to demonstrate being able to regulate their own negative feelings about their children's misbehaviors. Parents needs to model being safe-harbors during emotional storms. Parents do this by first showing the child how to calm down and then secondly, helping them to obey the rule and/or receive the consequence. Parents need to listen and administer justice while staying emotionally regulated and loving. This does not mean that parents need to deny or stuff feelings. It does mean that parents can say things such as "I am furious" and still behave in non-abusive and even compassionate ways.

There is no doubt that this is very challenging for parents, let alone, the immature minds of two year olds. It is, however, extraordinarily important work since it begins to lay down a foundation on which impulse control, distress tolerance and emotional regulation can be built. It takes years to build these skills. Skill levels will grow as the child's brain becomes more mature and complex. Parents facilitate this growth by firmly guiding children and lovingly giving them room to learn and practice.

When oppositional teens become dysregulated, it can be a very scary and destructive experience for all involved. Thus, it is very important that parents break the pattern of engaging in power struggles. This must be done by setting limits and consequences *collaboratively in advance* (see the balancing life section). It is also extremely important that parents model emotional regulation and actively listen to their dysregulated teens. Once rules have been established they must be *strictly and lovingly enforced* by parents.

Workbook Exercise – Loving and Firm

Describe the importance of parents modeling self-regulation to children.

_____

_____

_____

Describe the importance of being "safe and predictable"; even when children are acting out.

_____

_____

_____

Describe the problems that arise from negotiating with children when consequences should be delivered.

_____

_____

_____

Unconditional Love while being Strict Formula for Success

Since children need and yearn to be in right relationship with parents, it is critically important that they do not feel that their misbehaviors, errors in judgment, negative attitudes (including the infamous child "eye roll") and dysregulated emotions lead parents to stop loving them or devaluing them in anyway.

Addressing Negative Behaviors

However, this does not negate the fact that parents need to give consistent feedback about negative behaviors. Negative behaviors are unacceptable and warrant the consequences that have been previously and collaboratively formulated between parent and child. Parents must provide timely delivery of previously stated and agreed upon consequences. Parents need to be unwaveringly consistent in the delivery of consequences (a.k.a. strict).

Being strict is essential. Being strict does not mean being hard, rude, snide or unloving. Being strict means consistently doing what parents say they will do. It means that parents need to demand that behavior rules are obeyed and if not obeyed, the consequences are unequivocally enforced.

At the time of consequence delivery, parents must not spend energy justifying their motives or reasons for enforcing the consequences. They simply state the consequence and follow up with action. If parents start offering explanations, they will weaken the position that consequences must be enforced. Parents who offer explanations instead of the action needed to enforce the consequence, will inadvertently train children to debate them.

The time to explain the how, what, when, where and whys of rules is during family meetings. This is the place for parents and children to collaboratively create and discuss rules. Family meetings only occur during non-stressed/neutral times. Thus rules and consequences need to be decided in advance of any anticipated problem behaviors. This means parents need to get good at recognizing potential signs of developing problem behaviors.

Being strict does not require parents to use harsh tones or comments. In fact, the use of derogatory or shaming comments will backfire on the parents, since children will feel "wronged" and that the parent and entire world is unfair. When this happens, children are not able to internalize the very important notion that they made the wrong choice(s) (i.e. either to follow the rules or to receive consequence).

Delivering Consequences and Experiencing Repair

When parents firmly and lovingly deliver the consequences, they provide children the opportunity to accept the agreed upon consequence without creating or amplifying a relationship rupture. Compliance with the consequence allows the child to restore or repair the relationship. As soon as the child completes the age-appropriate consequence, the parent/child relationship must resume without a hitch. This means, the parent should not take any opportunity to shame or lecture since the consequence has already been served. Parents that lecture with "I told you so" will only end up shaming or enflaming children; this contributes to relationship ruptures. If the child is capable, willing and able and the "after-consequence delivery" situation and timing makes sense, the parent can lead an "active listening" discussion. This will help the child to process poor choices made and learn to better problem-solve. In such a case, the parent can use this time to increase closeness by increasing the understanding between parent and child.

Studies in attachment psychology (Arnold & Fisch, 2011) provide strong evidence that children need to experience "repairs" in relationships with parents. Relationship repairs allow children to become more emotionally regulated. This happens because children are able make sense of "what went wrong". They learn to accept feedback provided by parents. This allows children to increase their emotional complexity. Emotional complexity helps children to become better regulators of both their emotions and behaviors. This leads to being better problem-solvers when future challenges arise.

Thus, when parents deliver consequences in a loving, supportive and strict way, they are telling children that even though a problem exists, the problem is not big enough to separate the child from parent and not big enough to hurt their relationship. This allows children to feel and be motivated by the "thorn" of consequences but not be rendered "splat" by feelings of shame that arise as a result of feeling separated from a judgmental parent.

Crucial Learning from Mistakes

The ability to make a repair is crucial for children to be able to learn from their mistakes, poor judgments, and dysregulation. When children are able to internalize their decisions (i.e. choose to obey rule or get consequence), they develop greater self-control (includes emotional, behavioral, impulse control) and are more likely to develop genuine regret and sorrow for the impact their actions have on other people (however, this takes structural maturity of the brain which means parents must always be mindful of age-appropriate capacity).

Ruptures Hurt

When children are shamed, whether in a blatant or inadvertent manner, they experience psychological distress that overwhelms their capacities to calm themselves and overwhelms their capacities to organize the current experiences. When this happens, children are not in a position to learn from their mistake or make sense of the corrective attempts of the parent (particularly if parents reinforce the rupture in the relationship). However, there is still an even greater negative impact that results from maintaining or enlarging a relationship rupture; i.e. the overwhelming stress that children feel leads to disorganizing their existing coping structures (Arnold & Fisch, 2011). This means that repeated experiences of relationship ruptures with parents, leads to scaling down the emotional and cognitive complexity of children instead of building it up.

Parents need to be Reflective and Make Repairs Too

This does not mean that parents need to be "perfect". It does mean that parents need to work to be reflective of their own behaviors and be able to "catch" themselves when they are not acting in a manner that is consistent to maintain a healthy parent/child relationship. These are "oops" moments.

When a parent models saying "oops", they are conveying to children that people can self-correct. This is a wonderful life skill to demonstrate to children. It demonstrates, self-awareness, self-acceptance and problem-solving flexibility. This one syllable utterance signals that the parent has reflected on what was said and is reevaluating it. When a parent says "oops", it is good to follow it up with a repair statement such as "what I mean to say is...I am disappointed....or...I am angry about it and need to calm down" etc. Such statements are very powerful relationship repair vehicles. It helps to remove blame and judgment by applying "salve" on the relationship wound. Parents who say "sorry" and still enforce limits demonstrate that it is not about having to be "right" (power struggle dynamics) but about doing the right things (i.e. for the health and wellbeing of the child's developmental needs).

Workbook Exercise – Unconditional Love

Describe the qualities of being strict.

_____
_____
_____

Describe the qualities of being loving.

_____
_____
_____

Does being strict and loving go hand in hand?

_____
_____
_____

What impact does shame have on a child?

_____
_____
_____

What is the importance of making an emotional "repair"?

_____
_____
_____

Anxiety "Busting" Skills

Anxiety and Depression Patterns Can be Broken

No matter what you may have read or heard elsewhere, it is very important for parents to recognize that anxiety and depression are not genetically passed on traits. They are not parts of a person's personality. Anxiety and depression are the very real products that are created when people have dysfunctional life skills.

Anxiety Soup

In order to break out of the anxiety and/or depression "soup", one needs to recognize the types of thinking and behaviors that are key ingredients in the soup recipe. Here are the key anxiety making ingredients (ingredients also for depression; since anxiety typically is a pre-cursor to depression):

- **Global Thinking** (all or nothing)

- **Externalizing** (blaming others and acting as a victim)

- **Failure to compartmentalize** (failure to learn how to break down problems into manageable tasks)

- **Distress and frustration intolerance; no or little impulse control**

- **Failure to discriminate what to pay attention to and what to ignore** (e.g. failure to discriminate against critical inner voices; failure to recognize what is "in" or "out" of one's control)

- **Internal attribution** (i.e. internalizing the behaviors of others as "proof" that "I am defective")

- **Poor ability to self-regulate emotions; using maladaptive defenses**

- **Ineffective problem-solving skills**

Do these ingredients, by now, sound familiar? The answer should be – yes! These are the typical thought and behavior patterns of concrete and magical-thinking-age children. If children are not modeled healthy life skills by competent and loving adults, they will not learn to grow out of and dispel the anxiety-promoting cognitions and behaviors in the above list. Children must grow to understand that negative emotions and negative behaviors are not one and the same. The "anxiety ingredients" (all or nothing thinking; feeling as a victim; inability to tolerate distress and frustration) are typical of the concrete/magical thinking stage of development and so without guidance children might get "stuck" with these ineffective ways of interpreting and interacting with the world.

People "stuck" with anxiety-producing, ineffective life skills have a poor sense of personal agency. They do not recognize that people can separate how they feel from how they respond or react. Since people who utilize anxiety-producing life skills are more challenged to self-regulate and tolerate distress, they are more likely to be reactive rather than responsive when a problem arises. They justify their overreactions because they do not believe there is any choice. They do not realize that the degree to which a person acts out or stays calm has no bearing on how intensely a person feels inside. It is in fact the opposite, the degree that a person acts out is a direct report on how that person is unable to manage their feelings when a problem occurs.

Thus anti-anxiety skills means developing skills that are opposite to the "anxiety soup" ingredients listed above...

Confusing what "I do" with "what or who I am"

Some adults will say things such as "That's just how I am" or "I can't help it" (victim thinking)..."I am just an angry person" (labeling). When people make such statements, they are confusing "who they are" with "what they do" (or not do). When a person "acts out", this individual demonstrates not being able to respond to stress very well or in a competent, social manner. The person "loses it", "flips out", "feels overwhelmed" etc. because of not having learned the skills that would enable the person to respond.

Modeling Competence -Pausing, Looking and Making Choices

In reality, sometimes, even well regulated individuals will encounter challenging situations that feel "over-the-top". They may find, perhaps due to an accumulation of stress, these times are "too much to handle". During such a time, the regulating adult will recognize the possibility of being "pushed too far". This recognition signals to the competent adult that it is time to set a boundary and say "I can't do this right now". The overstressed person will then take the appropriate measures to do some self-care and delay tackling the problem until feeling more composed.

People are only able to correctly "size up" a situation (using discrimination and compartmentalization; these are "anti-anxiety skills") when they allow themselves to take time to pause and think before responding. People need to gather information in order to take the right actions to resolve the situation. Otherwise, people may reflexively react and thus, take the risk of "losing it" or "flipping out". It is highly probable that the situation will be made worse instead of improved when this happens (hence the world wants "First Responders" on the crisis scene rather than chaotic "First Reactors"; first reactors are indicative of poor impulse control, frustration and distress intolerance and poor emotional regulation).

Competence versus Perfection

And so, it needs to be noted that parents do not have to model perfection; rather, they need to model competence. They show competence when being able to respond or take a break as appropriate. These are important first steps in problem-solving and emotional regulation. Being responsible for one's own emotions; rather than personalizing; and being able to be accountable rather than externalizing and becoming a victim are also important skills that demonstrate competent decision-making. When parents do these things, they model emotional regulation to their children.

By now, it is likely that you recognize the helping children to problem-solve through active listening, setting healthy boundaries and modeling self-regulation are powerful ways to "bust" the anxiety soup ingredients listed earlier in this section. Active listening and problem solving help children build competence in addressing and handling life stresses. They will learn not to externalize and blame others; they will learn to size things up and break problems down into manageable sizes and workable solutions; learn problem-solving; set healthy boundaries; be able to discriminate about "what they will take and not take"; learn to emotionally regulate; and develop impulse control and distress/frustration tolerance.

In short, children who develop these skills will develop a strong sense of personal agency and this is *the antidote to anxiety and depression.*

Workbook Exercise – Anxiety Busting Formula

Describe the key ingredients that contribute to the development and maintenance of anxiety disorders.

_____

_____

_____

Describe the importance of parents modeling emotional regulation and competent problem solving for "busting" anxiety attitudes/thinking patterns.

_____

_____

_____

Describe how the parenting skills described in this workbook deflate anxiety thinking patterns.

_____

_____

_____

Realistic, Age-Appropriate Expectations for Balanced Life

In order to successfully extinguish behavioral patterns and dysfunctional cognitions that contribute to anxiety and depression (in both parents and children), parents need to be guided by realistic expectations (for self and other family members). Rigid and unrealistic expectations hurt everyone. They set people up for failure, shame and disappointment. Unrealistically high personal standards can also impact children in unexpected ways. In such a case, the inadvertent message given to children of parents with unrelenting standards is "you are not as good/competent/capable" as me (since the standard for me is higher than for you). Efforts made by parents to periodically reflect on one's standards and expectations can help put things back into a healthier balance.

Balancing Act – Structure, Nurture, Engagement

What parents *want* and what they can *expect from children* may be two different things. When wants and expectations are confused to be one and the same thing and they are actually out-of-alignment, people can end up feeling stymied, frustrated and disappointed.

Most parents *want* and *expect* their children to be well-behaved. The question is "Even though I want good behavior, can I realistically expect that my children will behave well?" "Global" statements such as "I want well-behaved children" need to be "compartmentalized". This means describing what "well-behaved" looks like for a child of a given age and given circumstances. It also means considering the capacities and limitations of the child. These considerations will help parents to construct a realistic plan with action steps so that the desired outcome of "well-behaved" can eventually be achieved.   It feels satisfying when "wants" and "expectations" are aligned.

To better align their "wants" and "expectations" for children, parents need to be mindful of what children need to be successful. Studies show (Booth &Jernberg) that children need: structure, nurturing and engagement. Parents who incorporate these elements into their interactions with children are likely to experience better behavioral outcomes and thereby reduce family stress.

Here are some examples of how parent can provide structure, nurturing and engagement in daily life:

- Respond to dysregulated children with a calming voice (*engagement*), a steadying touch or hug and gently rocking (*nurturing*) them. When parents reach out to a child in this way, the parent is helping the child to focus on the here and now; rather than on the internal distress (providing leadership and *structure* for the child). The parent is helping to "ground" (*nurture*) the child so that the parent's words (*engagement/leadership/structure*) will be heard and the parent's message (*guidance/structure*) received.

- Actively listening and using effective communication (*engaging*) such as "seems like" type of sentences are the tools parents use to "map" (*structure*) the child's experience so that the child better understands what is going on. For example, a parent may say, "Seems like you are so disappointed that you can't have that lollipop" (*provides a structure for experiencing feelings*). Suddenly, the child becomes aware and thinks some variation of "Oh, that is what I am...disappointed" (*feels understood; engaged*). Later, as the child's knowledge of words and emotions grow, the child may counter with "No, I am just frustrated that I have to wait".

Having realistic and age-appropriate expectations for behavioral outcomes reduces frustration level. In general, people suffer less when their expectations are more in line with reality. Parents who understand and appropriately respond to the emotional and cognitive capacities of children during the various stages of development; keep adult matters separate from children; watch out for "triangulation"; provide support and consistency; watch out for power struggles and stay on the lookout for other destructive dynamics will experience less frustration because they are *not wasting energy to pursue unrealistic outcomes*.

Other Considerations for Keeping Expectations Realistic

Misjudging a Child's Capabilities

When young children are able to articulate emotions, adults may *erroneously jump* to the opinion that the child is "super smart" or very precocious. In such a situation, it is likely the child has had the benefit of attentive parents or older siblings who helped

89

map the child's internal emotional experiences. The feelings have been connected to a label, the child has learned the label and so is able to be articulate it.

It is indeed great when young children are given the tools to articulate feelings; however, it is important for parents to realize that the size of a child's vocabulary or having success in articulating some feelings does not necessarily indicate that the child has an intellectual or emotional capacity greater what is possible at a particular age. It does, no doubt, suggest that the child is being intellectually stimulated (and, of course, this is very good for brain development). Parents need to remember that all human brains *need time to create* the structural growth that allows greater cognitive and affective capacity. When parents remember this, they will be less likely to misjudge and incorrectly elevate their child to an older mental age. Misjudging a child's mental age contributes to the misalignment of parental wants and expectations for the child (see previous section).

Unfair Burdens

Additionally, the artificial elevation of a child to an older mental age puts other unfair burdens on a developing child. This happens because of the foundational principle that children want "*nothing more than to please their parents*". And so, when parents expect the child to conform to the standards of an older child (mentally and emotionally), it is likely that the child will try to transform to be whatever the parents' expect. This will happen even though the child is unprepared for such a role.

Children who are expected to take on responsibilities and roles that are appropriate for older children become "parentified". Examples include: when a young child has to take care of younger siblings before having sufficient executive functions (these develop in teen years) or when a child needs to tend to the emotional needs of a dysregulated parent.

Inadvertently Setting Children Up for Failure

Children of all ages have *the capacity to learn* how to self-regulate and understand their feelings; however, it is important to remember that *competency takes time*. Since competency requires a mature brain and adequate skills training, it is better for parents to scale their expectations accordingly. Parents need to have realistic expectations as to what a child of a given age is truly capable of understanding (hence the repeated "age-appropriate" theme throughout this workbook). This helps parents set fair and reasonable limits and consequences for children.

When parents are realistic, they are less likely be among the type who *accidentally set children up for failure*. When children fail in pleasing parents, it is easy for them to internalize the relationship rupture as the "reality" that they are "no good" or "unlovable". This creates "internal attribution", a key ingredient for generating anxiety (see previous section on Anxiety Busting). A child's thwarted desire to stay in a right relationship with a parent along with the young child's immature brain and "magical thinking" contribute to this interior and perhaps private experience of feeling "less than". This means the child is left to his or her own immature resources to handle the distress; all of which may remain unknown to the parent. Realistic and responsive parents are less likely to contribute to the creation of this type of internalization.

Developmental Guidelines to Inform Expectations

Here are a few general guidelines to *inform your expectations* of children (Arnold & Frisch, 2011; Bowlby, 1988; Piaget, 1964) Note the italicized age-appropriate expectations in the paragraphs below:

- Infants are "undifferentiated" from their mothers (i.e. they do not have a sense of being an individual and *simply cry out to have their needs met;* they primitively begin to regulate when they learn to self-soothe when going to sleep); they *cannot be "spoiled"* and must have their needs met in a timely manner in order for a secure base of attachment to be established.

- Toddlers begin to gain a sense of self; a self with separate thoughts and opinions. *Their vocabulary, cognitions and ability to regulate are still very primitive. Shaming tactics are particularly overwhelming* to children of this age group. It is psychologically disorganizing. All developmental tasks are designed to make children become more complex; shaming is counter to this goal (and for older age brackets as well).

  Thus, toddlers, who have *very limited capabilities to self-regulate,* need parents to help them calm their bodies. They need a parent's soothing touch (nurture) and voice to feel physically and emotionally safe.

  Of course, age appropriate limits must also be set and enforced. A *consequence of 1 minute per year of age is appropriate.* Note: two minutes is an eternity to a toddler. In general, *any consequence longer than one minute per year of age will overwhelm the child's ability to cope* and will render them "splat". When children go "splat", they feel defeated. They feel helpless and blame parents and the world (notice how many "ingredients" from "anxiety soup" are present here). Treatment that renders children "splat" only serves to punish and is of no value for skill development (it does have "value" if the goal is to create "anxiety soup" or power struggles).

- Preschoolers are becoming more differentiated; however, *they still have difficulty with understanding complex concepts such as sharing and lying*. It is better to take a pre-emptive strike and eliminate situations that might require sharing (e.g. providing structure to make sure children have the same type of toy etc.) or by distracting children or engaging them with parent approved choices whenever possible. *Situations that involve lying warrant nothing further than simple statements* such as "we don't do that here". *The child should then be redirected*. Preschoolers need to be provided with *only a couple of choices* (that are appropriate to the situation and acceptable to the parent) so that they can feel personally empowered and less likely to engage in power struggles. Parents should not give endless choices as this will further frustrate the parents and the child.

- School age children are "magical thinkers" until growth in the executive centers of the brain ramps up. This acceleration in development begins at the onset of adolescence and continues to rev up through the teen years. The adult brain exists around the age of 25. School age children, do have an ever increasing capacity for complex thought and feelings, but *they are still relatively primitive thinkers*. This means: they are apt to "connect the dots" *with faulty logic* (e.g. "my parents are fighting... I feel bad...I must be bad"). As indicated in a previous section, parents typically have no awareness of the interior and private conclusions children are making. This means it is wise to *keep adults matters out of ear shot or vision of children*. Primary school children are "all or nothing" thinkers ("I always get it wrong"; "they are always unfair"; "they never listen to me") and *they are very concrete thinkers with limited capacity to understand more abstract concepts* (e.g. respect, appreciation, trustworthiness and so forth). As one can see, the capacities of this developmental stage are congruent with the ingredients that lead to anxiety and depression patterns. When parents are mindful of the vulnerabilities present in young children, they will be in a better position to remember how important it is to model more effective communication, coping and thinking skills.

- Teens *rapidly develop cognitive and emotional complexity*; however, they are also *more emotionally volatile due to the increased activation of the amygdala* portion of the brain (hence teens are greater risk takers even when their choices seem illogical). Teens greatly benefit from a parent who actively listens and collaboratively works with them to set limits and consequences (more on this later).

Summary on Setting Realistic Expectations

Having realistic and age-appropriate expectations for behavioral outcomes reduces frustration level. In general, people suffer less when their expectations are more in line with reality. Parents who understand and appropriately respond to the emotional and cognitive capacities of children during the various stages of development; keep adult matters separate from children; watch out for "triangulation"; provide support and consistency; watch out for power struggles and stay on the lookout for other destructive dynamics will experience less frustration because they are *not wasting energy to pursue unrealistic outcomes*.

Regardless of the stage of maturity, all children need parents to model emotional regulation; competent problem-solving (not perfection); actively listen so as to help children benefit from social regulation of emotions (and consequently build distress tolerance and build self-regulation and impulse control); and set age appropriate limits and consequences (which are predictably enforced). It *is hugely unrealistic* to expect that children will not balk (publicly or privately) when parents hold children to higher standards than applied to the parents. This leads to children feeling that such a parent (and even the world) is unfair (providing more ingredients for "anxiety soup").

Workbook Exercise – Age Appropriate Expectations

T or F

Children in the same family should be treated the same way (regardless of age) because it is "fair".

Teen age years are especially challenging because of increased amygdala activation.

Children need to respect and appreciate parents or else they are "spoiled".

Children need parents to demonstrate emotional regulation.

Children benefit most from perfect parents.

Further Balancing Measures - Keeping Expectations Real

Keep a Wall between Adult matters and Children

Children are accidentally harmed by parents when there is no wall of separation between adult matters and those of concern to children. The degree of harm created will depend on the age of the child and the degree of distress produced by the adult content material.

Even when children insist that they are coping or understand, a wise parent will remember that children do not have the cognitive and emotional capacity to deal with complex adult issues. As mentioned in the previous section about "Expectations", it is unfair to burden children with adult matters (especially pinning one parent against another). Parents who purposely or accidentally involve children in adult matters, inadvertently rob them of precious emotional and cognitive resources which are better spent on important child development issues.

Parents should never treat a child as a "friend" (not possible or fair to the child until an adult brain is present around age 25). This breaches the "wall of separation" too. Parents should never use children as "confidantes". They should never assign children tasks or grant privileges that are not appropriate for their ages (even when children insist that "I am old enough"; e.g. dating at an early age).

Workbook Exercise – Separate Matters

T or F

"Cool parents" befriend their teenagers.

Parents should always consider the age-appropriateness of the child and keep adult type concerns separate from children.

_____

_____

_____

Give 2 examples of simplified explanations of adult matters (appropriate to age).

94

_____

_____

_____

_____

_____

_____

What else can adults do to help children feel safe when adults are challenged by significant problems?

_____

_____

_____

Communicate Unity with other Parent

In the interest of creating a harmonious and safe home environment, it is extremely important for parents to represent their relationship as one of agreement and mutual respect. This will help parents avoid sending mixed and confusing signals to children. It will also prevent children from trying to pit one parent (triangulation) against the other as they attempt to align themselves with the parent who agrees with them.

Since children benefit when parents present a united front, it makes sense for parents to develop their house rules; parenting styles and value system separately from children. Parents need, in some cases, agree to disagree with each other; however, they need to be consistent when presenting to children what has reached agreement.

Whenever an issue arises in front of the children that presents "new ground", parents have an opportunity to model good problem solving skills. Parents can do this by simply saying: "I do not know"… "I will need to think about it"… "We will need to continue this conversation when I/we have a chance to think about it more"…. "I don't know….I want to see what your father/mother has to say" (this is different than threatening a child with "wait 'til your father gets home)…. "I need more information before I can say" and so forth.

When children are impatient and distressed about having to wait for an answer, parents can work with the children to build distress tolerance. Parents can use active

95

listening skills to help children map their feelings and arrive at ways they can calm themselves while they wait for an answer.

Workbook Exercise – Communicating Unity

Describe a problem that can arise when parents disagree in front of children.

_____

_____

_____

Describe triangulation and what problems may arise from it.

_____

_____

_____

Take an Active, Supportive Interest

People feel connected and important when other people take an interest in them. This is especially true for children since they yearn to be in good relationship with their parents and other family members. Whether children are describing problems or talking about their lives, *it is important to remember names of friends and the details of events and things that are important to them.* When you make reference to these details in a future conversation, children will be impressed that you listened and remembered. This tells them that they are important enough to pay attention to and that you really care about them. It creates a shared history which is very bonding. Contrast this to any personal experiences you may have when you have had to repeat what you say and still not feel heard.

Workbook Exercise – Take an Active Interest

Describe why it is important to take an active interest in your child's world.

_____

_____

_____

Describe what not to do when listening to a child's perspective.

_____

_____

_____

Always Do What You Say You Will Do

When parents do as they say they will do, they are putting actions behind their words. This is very important because it trains children that you are worthy of trust. It will also lead them to respect you. Parents need to realize that qualities such as trust and respect are earned (even by parents) and not granted due to rank. When parents demand respect, children may seem to comply; however, the parent is really ruling by fear. This means that when the parent is not present, the children may disobey and/or express their true sentiments. When parents act in respect and trustworthy ways, children will always feel confident and able to rely on what parents say. When parents always deliver what they say in a loving way, parents tell children that their home environment is safe and predictable; even when the outside world is not. This is a wonderful gift to give to children.

A mistake that parents commonly make is when they are random with consequences. Random consequences are usually invented on the spur of the moment (and so are dependent upon the current mood of the parent). The parent may change previously outlined consequences or fail to do what they originally stated they would do (perhaps after "giving in" to the child's efforts to negotiate). When parents make these random alterations, they give children the accidental message that the world is unpredictable and subject to mood swings. Such messages are in direct contrast to the "Good parent" mission to help children regulate their emotions, manage impulses and exercise self-discipline. Parent randomness teaches children to be reactive instead of learning how to appropriately respond. It contributes to the building of anxiety ingredients (see previous section about anxiety).

Workbook Exercise – Do What You Say

Describe the importance of creating a safe and predictable home environment for children.

_____

_____

_____

Describe the impact of parental mood swings on children.

_____

_____

_____

Describe how to make a "repair" when parental reactions create unsafe feelings for children.

_____

_____

_____

Imbalances Fuel Power Struggles

Power struggles are at the center of many dysfunctional relationships so it is worthwhile to explore them further.

Characteristics of Power Struggles

Power struggles are easy to define; however, they are not always easy to identify. Power struggles are particularly hard to identify when someone is immersed in one. It is far easier for a neutral observer to recognize when it is occurring. This is because those who are in power struggles have emotionally vested interest in "winning" a certain outcome. Heightened emotion and determination to achieve a desired outcome lead people to justify the tactics they use; even when this means using ineffective communication techniques that alienate other people and create unhealthy imbalances in family relationships.

Ineffective communication techniques that contribute to power struggle dynamics include: blaming; shaming; labeling; talking over someone else; not actively listening; judging; all or nothing and catastrophizing remarks; and sarcasm and ridicule. It also includes yelling and other behaviors that indicate a person has become dysregulated.

Imbalances in the Family Universe

The very nature of a power struggle creates an imbalance where there is a "winner" and therefore also a "loser". The reality is, of course, that no one in a loving relationship truly wins a power struggle. This is because when someone "loses", the overall relationship suffers. The winner and loser continue to feel less connected as resentment may build up in the heart of the "loser".

Young children are quite easily made to be the "losers" because parents are typically physically, intellectually and emotionally stronger. Parents control the finances. Parents can easily dictate to children what they can and cannot do. This may feel like the correct order of the universe to parents; however, to children who have little control, it can feel like bullying. It also feels unfair and leads children to feel that they are helpless victims (victims are prone to anxiety; see "anxiety soup" section). When parents remember that their real mission is to help children become confident and competent life problem-solvers, they can become mindful of how contributing to children's feelings of helplessness is counterproductive.

The goal is to help children feel empowered to make the right decisions. Power struggles do not contribute to the healthy empowerment of children. They do lead to children fighting to arrest power from their parents; after all, it is natural for people to put up some sort of fight when "drowning". Ultimately power struggles lead to either defeated children or oppositional children (depending whether the child has a compliant or more demanding type of temperament).

Telltale Signs

When parents engage in power struggles, it is common for such parents to feel dismay and confusion about "what in the world they can do" in lieu of power tactics. Such parents believe it means "handing" control over to the children. They can think of no other parenting alternatives. However, upon closer examination, most parents who engage in power struggles will soon realize that being in a power struggle signals that control has already been lost (since so much of the child's energy is being spent defying the parent instead of complying with the rules). Whenever a parent feels afraid that the children will "rule", then it is safe to say that this parent engages in power struggle dynamics.

Although power struggles may commonly involve overt signs of disagreement such as yelling, power struggles may exist even when there are no overt fights and someone is simply quietly and inflexibly resisting. Whether a power struggle is blatant or insidious, the common theme is that one person's will attempts to overpower the other person's will.

The overpowered person feels helpless and that the *world is "unfair"* (externalization is a key ingredient in developing "anxiety soup"). When children utter the word *"unfair",* parents should do a quick review to see if a power struggle occurred. Parents will confirm that a power struggle took place if the parent randomly "pulled rank" instead of enforcing limits/rules as they were previously stated to the child. When children feel that the world is "unfair", they are basically *blaming* others instead of holding themselves accountable (more discussion will be given in an upcoming section about how to set limits and consequences in a fashion that helps children become accountable instead of resentful and helpless; feelings of helplessness contribute to and perpetuate anxiety).

Imbalances Arising from Excessive Praise

Methods to boost self-esteem and confidence that rely on external, inflated praise are frequently used by parents and both public and private schools. There are very many schools that place signage to announce "the world's best students go here". This and other such proclamations are at best meaningless and at worse tell children they do not have to do anything to warrant such praise. As bad as this seems, it can be worse yet. It is worse when a child does not feel comfortable or able to align self with the school's pronounced culture of being the "best". This contributes to the child feeling as a "misfit" or "defective".

Excessive external praise teaches children to *seek the approval* of others in order to feel okay about themselves (*and therefore it becomes even more important to win and be right in power struggles*). This is particularly problematic when children become teens. Teens who have been taught to seek the approval of others will find it even more difficult to set boundaries with their peers. It is far better to help children develop an inner sense of competence as effective and flexible problem solvers. Parents can also help children focus on internal feelings of satisfaction about jobs well done. This is as simple as asking a child "How does it feel to get that done?" or "What lovely colors you chose...what led you to pick them?" This will generate genuine feelings of confidence and self-esteem and this increases the probability that healthy boundaries will be set and defended during difficult situations.

A Variety of Temperaments – Oppositional Defiance Revisited

The power struggle dynamic is also very problematic because it is a key ingredient leading to the creation of oppositional defiance. Oppositional defiance is the term used to describe children who have developed "ungovernable behaviors". It is common for people to mistakenly believe that oppositional children are "just born that way" or that it is "in their temperament". This interpretation of oppositional is a sort of "blame the victim" type of stance; i.e. parents externalizing the difficulties that arise from their parenting choices and placing the blame on children who have little control or choice. While it is true that some children have more "fussy" or "challenging" temperaments, it is not true that this leads to oppositional behaviors. The truth about oppositional behaviors is that they represent the ultimate need to "win" a power struggle "at all or any cost". This stems from not feeling heard, feeling unimportant and feeling dismissed (not from temperament). Clearly, there are no winners.

Children who resort to oppositional behaviors do so because they have not been guided to develop distress tolerance, emotional regulation or a sense of accountability. When oppositional children have their wills thwarted, they fall into the only "skill set" they have; i.e. *the power struggle*. They will continue to "up the ante" (i.e. the opposition) until it finally "pays off" (i.e. they get what is wanted). The "winning" of the power struggle trains children to continue to engage in them.

The more years that a child has "invested" in using oppositional behavior, the greater the family imbalances and the more extreme the behaviors are likely to get. This means that the power struggle continues even though parents try harsher and harsher punishments. The harsh punishments become less and less effect in controlling the child's behaviors.

It is sad, but true. Many oppositional children's behaviors become so extreme that they become repeat offenders in the criminal justice system; yet, even this does not deter them. When children end up seeing themselves as "bad" or "defective" rather than poorly skilled in emotional regulation and impulse control, it becomes very hard to turn against maladaptive strategies. Fortunately, change is still possible. The parenting framework has been successfully used in correctional and residential settings.

.

Workbook Exercise – Power Struggles

Describe the destructive impact of power struggles.

_____
_____
_____

What constitutes a power struggles?

_____
_____
_____

Alternate Paths –Eliminating Power Struggles

Active listening and guiding with questions to help children problem-solve are very powerful tools that help eliminate power struggles. This is because the parent takes on the role of a kind and benevolent mentor who is interested in helping children resolve their perceived problems. There is no rupture in the relationship since the parent and child are on the "same side"; i.e. to solve the problem. It is extremely important to note that the mentor "helps the child do the work to solve the problem" rather than fixing it for the child.

A kind and benevolent mentor:

- Understands the child

- Loves the child

- Wants the child to become a competent problem-solver and self-disciplined person.

This means that, when necessary, the parent/mentor must set limits and deliver consequences; however, the rules and consequences need to have been stated to the child in advance (more on this skill in an upcoming section).

Thus it is very useful and affirming to use active listening to engage children. When used to address problems it is a collaborative approach. When children are asked "what" and "how" questions, they are actively involved in solving their dilemmas. This is a very powerful skill building exercise for children that contributes to high levels of confidence and self-esteem. It is much more effective for building an authentic and internal sense of confidence and self-esteem then methods that rely on excessively praising children.

Summary

So what does "The Good Parent" need to do to eliminate power struggles? The answer is simple: Create healthy balances. Do this by:

- Actively listening to children

- Being a flexible, loving, guiding parent who sets and enforces limits

- Be more interested in solving problems than being right.

Workbook Exercise – Eliminating Power Struggles

Describe an effective means to eliminate power struggles.

_____

_____

_____

What are some qualities that help dissolve power struggles?

_____

_____

_____

_____

_____

_____

Describe the importance of developing a child's internal sense of control and well-being.

_____

_____

_____

Parent Reflections – Rebalancing Unrealistic Expectations

Parent Roles

Helping children develop emotional regulation so they can lead full lives as competent problem-solvers and authentic people is no small task. It is indeed, an enormously large and important task.

Parents Need to Self-Reflect

The child raising task is so important that it warrants parents taking time to look at themselves. This includes looking at their own attachment styles, any issues they have with their attachment and any unrealistic expectations that may have developed as a result of their attachment style (parents should listen to the audio portion that is available with this workbook; the instructions for accessing the MP3s are at the end of Appendix A).

When parents consider "what worked" and "what was problematic" for them as children, they can begin to increase self-awareness about the origin of their own communication and coping styles. Parents who can self-reflect are more apt to stop using styles of parenting that were "handed to them".

It is important to note that reflecting on "what worked" and "what did not work" is not about blame. It is not about blaming this generation of parents or about blaming their parents or blaming the ones before them. Blaming is a useless activity for children and adults. It leaves one feeling as a victim (and thus helpless) and it wounds those being blamed. Rather reflection is meant to help people increase self-awareness so one can better understand how one "arrived" at where one is now. People cannot make change if they continue to view themselves as helpless or hopeless or act clueless about the things they do.

It is also very important for people to realize that self-reflection helps people discover the things *they do* rather than about making an assessment of *"who they are"*. People can change what they do (even changing challenging and entrenched habits). When people think that learned patterns of anxiety, depression, anger, "losing it", avoidance or any other maladaptive defense, reflect "who they are", the will feel helpless and stuck. It is much more productive and healthier to focus on what one needs to do to make change.

Courageous Parents

Self-awareness is fundamental to making changes of any sort; however, it can often be an uncomfortable or even distressing process to reflect upon one's mistakes. It is temporarily easier to use avoidance strategies; however, this only leads to the problem remaining unsolved and perhaps getting worse. It takes effort to stop the transmission of dysfunctional communication and coping patterns from one generation to the next.

Some changes may be very difficult for parents to make on their own. Behaviors and attitudes that were created in childhood become entrenched habits and may require objective feedback from a neutral party. A goal with a neutral party might be to identify dysfunctional coping and communication methods in order to begin making change. A neutral party may be an active listener or a professional therapist. The discussion should not be a venting session. Venting is all about blaming and leaves people feeling worse off and helpless.

Whenever parents decide to work on building more effective emotional regulation, impulse control, emotional intimacy, confidence, healthy boundaries and other qualities, they move toward being better role models and exerting greater positive influence on their children. Children benefit from the work parents do to address problematic issues. Not only will children benefit, but the parent who is making changes and any adult relationships this parent has will benefit as well.

Strong Role Models

Whenever parents work on making positive changes in their lives, even when the path is slow and grinding, they present as strong and positive role models to children. It takes a lot of courage to self-reflect and identify areas that need change. This is because self-reflection involves seeing and hearing things people would simply prefer not to see or hear.

Natural Interference

There is also a natural tendency of human brains which make examining one's self a little hard. The tendency is that all human brains want to hone in on "evidence" that supports what they already believe to be true (while ignoring anything that contradicts what is already believed) (Wilson, 2011). This tendency stems from the automatic nonverbal survival efforts of all human brains. This active subconscious portion contains computer-like "scripts" that were formed throughout childhood. These scripts or "schemas" inform our actions (and reactions) and lead people to behave in ways that may seem puzzling; even to themselves. It takes critically thinking brains to stop it.

So in order to cultivate a responsive conscious mind, a person needs to "step-back" and ask "what" and "how questions" (about self and others). When parents model this "stepping-back", even when struggling with it, they become strong role models for accepting and using feedback. Children will also see their parents as powerful role models for growth and change (instead of needing to be "right" and consequently "stuck").

Role Models do not need to Over Explain

Being role models means parents can minimize the use of words because their actions are speaking volumes. When parents model accepting feedback and being self-evaluative, they do not have to justify, self-criticize or evaluate themselves to the children. It is very important that parents maintain their leadership role and avoid accidentally elevating children to the status of "little adults" by "explaining too much". Parents need to remember the concept of the "good enough parent" (Winnicott, 1964). Such a parent can accept feedback but also model competent problem solving.

This means that parents are to give age-appropriate, *concise answers* that keep that "wall of separation" in tact between adult matters and those of children (no over-explaining). Parents who use "oops" or make statements such as "that is something I will need to consider further" or "I feel sort of cranky and need to chill before I can discuss it" are keeping the wall of separation between adults and children. This is important to do because children are not emotionally or cognitively complex enough to handle any concerns that include wondering if their caregiver is able of "taking care of it".

Parents Hold It Together

Children basically need and want their worlds to be safe and predictable. They need their parents to "hold it together" even when there are intense problems to be solved. Sometimes a reassuring "I will figure something out" is enough; even when there are financial woes or other things of significant life-impacting magnitude.

Parents Need Life Skills

If parents do not know how to address their own problems or emotional needs, they will spill it over the "wall of separation" and children will be unfairly burdened by it. If parents are able to recognize that their problems are spilling over, they need to figure out how to stop doing it or get outside help to address their concerns.

On the flip side, children also benefit when parents do not "stuff" their feelings. No one can truly "stuff it" for long before an explosion, resentment or other type of "spilling over the wall" occurs. This is why parents need to become good at recognizing and appropriately meeting their own needs.

(Please utilize the auditory portion of this workbook to bolster your skills; see Appendix A for instructions)

Predictable Parents

When parents are able to address their own issues and keep them separate from the lives of children, they will be better able to provide the safe and predictable environments that children need. Safe and predictable environments are "good enough" environments; not perfect ones. Safe and predictable environments have limits and consequences that do not come out of "thin air". Safe and predictable environments do not suddenly "flip" based on the mood swings of parents or any unexpected turn of event.

When the safety and predictability of a home environment does change with a parental mood swing, the accidental message given to children is that the parent does not have ability to exercise self-control either. Children will wonder about expectations placed on them to demonstrate internal emotional and behavioral control when their parents are out of control themselves (especially when parents "lose it" by yelling, using aggressive words and behaviors and so forth). This is indeed a double standard which does get noticed by children. Children, who see this double standard, will believe that their world is "unfair".

Important Reasons for Considering Parent Development

There are so many negative outcomes that can result from parents not being able to regulate themselves; these include: children who are left to their own emotional resources to soothe themselves (which are limited due to the immature nature of their brains); children feeling emotional isolated; children feeling afraid; children not trusting adults; children copying dysregulated behaviors and believing that these behaviors are "normal". Additionally, children will not be on track to further age-appropriate development.

All of these outcomes negatively impact the developing skill sets of a child. Children with weakened coping and communication skills are more likely than children who have strong developmental foundations to have ongoing difficulties. These difficulties will extend from the present through any remaining developmental stages into adulthood.

Achieving Good Balance; Being Responsive

When safety and predictability are kept in good balance by parents (who model competent problem-solving and do not over-explain themselves to children), children will have the opportunity to work on the appropriate developmental tasks at hand. Parents who keep a safe and predictable home environment effectively show children that problems can be managed (one way or another) by being responsive rather than out-of-control and reactive (which is very destabilizing and scary to children as well as other adults). Responsive parents show children that the external world may pose problems, but the internal problem-solving and coping abilities of a parent can sort it out, make sense of it and organize it.

Parents who are responsive and effective problem-solvers begin to show children that there are things in the world that are "outside of one's control" and other things that are "inside of one's control". This is a very crucial distinction for children to make as it will help them organize their worlds into "problem-solving bites"; i.e. according to what is within or outside their abilities to influence. Such skill helps children avoid the development of "all or nothing" thinking and "catastrophizing". All or nothing thinking and catastrophizing are chief components in the development of anxiety and depression disorders (see "anxiety soup" section). When all or nothing and catastrophizing become habitual ways of interacting with the world, children start to believe that this is "who I am" (i.e. an "anxious" or "depressed" person) instead of this is "what I have learned to do".

Rules for Creating a Safe and Predictable Environment for Family Life

When parents create a safe and predictable environment, children are allowed to develop accountability. Safe and predictable environments are created when:

- Parents are responsive to children and consistent with their own behaviors.

- Rules and consequences are made known to children in advance of an infractions; rules and consequences are not arbitrary.

It is best when rules are created collaboratively at a family meeting.

Family Meeting System for Rule and Consequence Creation

- Parents identify that their child is having difficulty completing tasks, regulating, or doing any of the life skills discussed in this workbook.

- Parents take the opportunity to hold a family meeting to problem-solve with the child having the problem.

- Parents need to approach the child having the problem in a safe and supportive way to call attention to the issue. The parent summarizes the perceived problem and proposes that a meeting is held to work on the problem.

- The parent uses language that demonstrates a desire to support the child in learning new ways to solve the problem. As examples, parents might say, "I notice that you seem to be having difficulty completing your homework before bedtime....I wonder how I can help you find ways to get it done... so that I won't keep telling and nagging about it". "Let's sit down for a few minutes and figure out a plan".

- Family meetings can be comprised of any number of people. Typically, the meetings involve the children who are involved with the identified problem. In a situation that only involves one child, it is probably not appropriate to have siblings present at the meeting. The parent and the child with the identified problem can collaboratively work out a plan for change (includes rules and incentives/consequences).

- At every family meeting, parents encourage children to contribute their ideas to make very specific plans. This means the plans include: "how, what, when, where, and when" details. This is done so there are no "loop holes" that contribute to misunderstandings and protests when, at a later times, the rules are not followed and consequences need to be enforced.

- Parents take a leadership role and guide children; helping children to contribute better/more realistic ideas for rules (through active listening and questioning).

- When the rules are created, parents recap the rule and ask if the child understands the rule, if the child agrees with how it has been recapped, and if the child has any questions.

- The child will then confirm that this is indeed the rule that was created jointly.

- When the rule is confirmed, the parent and child follow the same procedure for consequence creation. Parents should once again guide children on age-appropriate consequences (usually one minute per age of child). Remember the goal is to create an incentive for children to choose to comply with the rule; i.e. learn impulse control and accountability; not to dishearten the child with punishments that render the child "splat".

When children are first invited to participate in the creation of rules and consequences, they at first may be hesitant to contribute their ideas. They also tend to scoff at the notion of creating consequences and try to assign minimal and inappropriate ones. However, after a few family meetings are held, children start to be more active, informed and appropriate participants. Family meetings only need to take a few minutes; they may be scheduled or held spontaneously to attend to identified problem behaviors.

Value of the Family Meeting System

When consequences are predictably delivered, children learn to have an "internal locus of control". This means children begin to recognize that the consequences are a direct result of choices made by them. It means that even though children do not like the consequence, they can see the cause and effect and therefore do not lament that it is "unfair". The world may be difficult, but children will start to realize that their choices do impact the way they experience it.

Collaboratively Generating Rules and Consequences has Benefits

- Parent and child collaboratively generate rules in agreement with the family value system and parents' judgment. *Children learn the family values.*

- Parent and child generate and agree upon consequences (in agreement with the

110

family value system and parents' judgment). *Children are being given the opportunity to develop internal control and self-discipline.*

- When children realize that they consistently get the agreed upon consequence when the agreed upon rule is violated, *children learn self-discipline* and feel empowered because they can choose not to break the rule.

- When parents consistently hold children responsible for complying with the collaboratively made rules and doing the agreed upon tasks, parents are freed from having to "nag". *Children feel competent and accountable.* They begin to learn to "put the brakes" on their own behaviors; even when it is hard or emotionally unpleasant.

Distress and Frustration Tolerance Boosted

This process of doing something which is hard "even when it stinks" fosters both distress tolerance and self-discipline. The ability to tolerate distress and still be able to forge on in a responsive way is crucial for effective and competent problem-solving. The ability to discipline oneself is crucial for developing so many other life skills; including but not limited to: doing well in school, achieving in sports, learning a job; working through problems in relationships and succeeding in any endeavor that is challenging.

Workbook Exercise – Creating Balance

Describe the importance of parents demonstrating emotional regulation.

_____

_____

_____

What role does distress tolerance play for parents?

_____

_____

_____

Describe the Family Meeting System. What is the key components that determine whether the system is successful or not?

_____

_____

_____

What life skills does the family meeting system help children develop?

_____

_____

_____

Why is creating a safe and predictable environment important? How can it be created?

_____

_____

_____

_____

_____

_____

The Parenting Framework

Long Summary

1. The goal is to be a "good enough parent" (first coined as the "good enough mother" in 1953 by British pediatrician and psychoanalyst, Donald Winnicott) (Winnicott, 1964). The "good enough parent" means being a parent who is not "hung up" on unrealistic standards or defensively tries to be "perfect". The "good enough" parent can flexibly model effective problem-solving; healthy coping; and is able to increase emotional connections by actively listening to feelings. The "good enough parent" helps children build self-efficacy, personal empowerment and an optimistic outlook on life. This parent helps children learn how to effectively deal with the realities of an imperfect world and the uncertainties that accompany it.

    Children benefit from the "good enough parent" because such a parent can set healthy limits and reevaluate "what works" and "what does not work" and can accept feedback to adjust accordingly. All of these are very powerful and life affirming skills that the "good enough parent" gives to a child in his or her care. These skills are powerful "inoculations" against the development of anxiety and depression syndromes that are now plaguing the world (the World Health Organization lists depression as the 2nd leading health cause of human suffering) (Yapko, 2009).

2. The "good enough parent" knows that children need to have their developmental needs considered and responded to accordingly. Over-explaining to children has the accidental impact of elevating them to "little adults" and this is developmentally stressful and unfair to children (their emotional IQ and brain structure cannot accommodate this type of demand). Children who appear to be "7 going on 13", "11 going on 20" or any other variation of this theme, are likely to be acting from inadvertent "training" by the adults who care for them. Children who have responsibilities that are beyond their developmental capacities suffer the risk of being "parentified".

    When children's developmental needs are not met, they are inadvertently being set up for all kinds of mental health distress; depending on the severity of the failure to address developmental needs, this may include: major anxiety; depression (anxiety in children is a significant predictor of major depression in as little as 8 years after the onset of anxiety); somatic manifestations of distress (including migraines, fibromyalgia, irritable bowel syndrome and more); addictions; oppositional defiance; conduct disorders and personality disorders (e.g. borderline personality disorder). Inadvertently elevating children to "little adult status" invites them to negotiate with parents (as they are inadvertently begin to see themselves as "peers" to parents) and externalize their unmet desires; i.e. blaming parents and viewing the world as "unfairly against them". This type of communication dynamic leads to destructive power struggle cycles.

3. The "good enough parent" knows that children thrive when parents operate as "kind and benevolent" rulers; i.e. as a monarchy rather than a democracy (which invites children to be "little adults"). Parents as kind and loving monarchs get to provide direction according to their own value system and also set limits according to these values. Such parents are willing to listen to the "petitions" of their children and collaboratively guide children through rule-making and problem solving (and thus help children build impulse control, critical thinking, emotional regulation and accountability).

When parents predictably utilize the rules and consequences that were collaboratively set with children during a family meeting, children learn to view parents as fair and trustworthy (i.e. parents deliver what was agreed upon at the family meeting). When parents deliver the consequences in a matter-of-fact or even a compassionate nature (but still do not entertain negotiations), children learn that they can make mistakes, act out, and use poor judgment without falling out of relationship with parents; i.e. they do not view themselves as "defective"; rather they recognize that they are responsible for the choices they make.

4. The "good enough parent" recognizes that developmentally appropriate family meetings are held to address skill deficits and support ongoing skill development; this is the best way to create a safe and predictable home environment. Such parents have age-appropriate expectations of children; i.e. parents recognize that children are not yet good at impulse control and emotional regulation. This means when children have difficulties, parents need to remember that children are feeling challenged rather than being "bratty" or "manipulating" (productive family meetings address the identified problem behavior by creating guidelines for change via rule and consequence generation). The introduction of the family meeting "agenda" needs to be done in a way that affirms the child's difficulty; i.e. with the purpose of creating a plan to help the child build the skill(s) needed (rather than coercing with shame or

personal attacks).

5. Parents can hold spontaneous family meetings (e.g. to address an ongoing or recently identified important concern) and/or have regularly scheduled meetings. During the regularly scheduled meetings, children may be encouraged by parents to bring up any concerns or complaints they may have. Family meetings are the appropriate forum to re-evaluate any rules or consequences that were previously made (note: rules/consequences never get re-evaluated at the time the consequence is to be delivered). For example, a parent might use "I" messages to say "I notice that you seem to be having difficulty keeping your room organized/clean etc.....and I thought it would be good for us to sit down and figure out a way that will help you take care of your things better". If and when children protest, parents can actively listen to feelings but stick to the task at hand (i.e. having the family meeting).

   Parents need to be mindful of other activities or other expectations that children have so that the calling of the family meeting is not viewed as "unfair" (this is the advantage of having regularly scheduled meetings). Parents might even consider setting ground rules around family meetings (e.g. children can request to have one scheduled if they want to review rules/consequences or problem solve).

6. During the family meeting, parents identify the topic/problem that needs to be addressed and invites the child/children to offer input. The parent(s) then actively listen and use "how" and "what" questions to help the child/children problem-solve and consider the outcomes of any faulty logic they suggest. When parents actively listen and respond sensitively to children's feelings, perspectives, opinions, and faulty logic (via "how" and "what" questions, and "seems like"/"sounds like" statements), children will develop problem-solving skill while feeling heard and connected to parents.

   Parents need to guide children into establishing a sequence (how, what, when, where) of tasks/steps that will define the rule being made. When the rule is decided, parents recap everything decided and then ask the children whether they understand or have any questions. This process is repeated for the consequence portion of the family meeting.

   When the rules and consequences are decided, parents will help children become more accountable by recapping both rules and related consequences one more time. Once again, parents need to ask children whether they have any questions (this step is very important because it is highly likely that children will protest at the first enforcement of the consequence by crying "unfair"; when this happens, a parent simply needs to say something such as "Oh, you agreed that this was the way things were to be.....next time, you will need to choose better".

7. Parents must always deliver the consequences that were decided in the family meeting (otherwise the system collapses and such a parent trains children that the parent is not trustworthy and also not worthy of respect). Parents must demonstrate that they will predictably, safely and compassionately deliver the consequence (this means that you do not demean the child with scary/angry/pouty/callous/cold language; rather you simply enforce the terms previously set).

It is important for parents to remember that they are policing behaviors not emotions. Children are likely to be upset, angry, frustrated, sad and crying; however, if they are complying with the consequence and not acting out, the lessons are being learned. After the consequence is completed as previously determined, parents can help children process the feelings that they had as they experienced the consequence. Discussion after the consequence, follows the same format; i.e. parents use active listening and guide with appropriate questions to help the child understand self and be understood by parents. Remember, parents do not have to agree with children when they actively listen. It is important not to try to fix or dismiss children's feelings (e.g. "It was not that bad"; rather say "Sounds like you were angry....what did you do to calm yourself?").

8. "Good enough parents" need to model impulse control, emotional regulation, effective-problem solving and good decision making. For example, when a parent is cranky or perhaps unavailable due to a conflicting demand, the parent can say such things as "I can't do this now.....I need to take some time to relax.....let's talk after dinner.......or.....oops.....I didn't mean to say that....what I meant to say was this.....oops....I am sorry....what I meant to do was.......I need to take a few minutes to wind down" etc. "Good enough parents" police their own behaviors; i.e. they catch and stop themselves from yelling or doing anything else that suggests a "double standard" (remember children will do what they see and hear; additionally, parents cannot hold a child to a higher standard than they have for themselves...children will view this as "unfair"....and it certainly is; especially when you consider that children do not have the executive brain functions that adults have).

9. Rules and consequences must always be age-appropriate and need to change to better match the growing child and situation (but never make changes at the

time of consequence delivery; all changes are made at family meetings). Consequences are best when they tied to the misbehavior and are delivered immediately. This is why parents are advised to let children know that the consequences can be delivered anywhere; however, when you are in a public place or the children's friends are present, you need to be discrete. Humiliating your child is counterproductive. Find a way to deliver without shaming.

10. Parents must always keep adult matters separate from children; this means making sure that children are out of earshot of adult discussions. Parents must create a unified front for children. They may have "secret signals" to send to each other to support the other parent and help each other "stay in check" when in front of the children. Even divorced parents need to do it. If one divorced parent is not mindful of these considerations, the mindful parent still needs to make sure that the child is not accidentally "pulled in" to the "right" parent's side. The mindful parent needs to continue to assert the boundary between adults and children by saying simple statements such as "This is for grownups to worry about.....I will handle it" or "we don't do that here" (if parents are in separate households).

Short-Cut Summary

1. Parents do not need to be perfect, just "good enough" and work to demonstrate effective problem-solving, impulse control, emotional regulation, coping and active listening.

2. Parents need to respond appropriately to their children's developmental needs; this means not making demands that are inappropriate to a child's age and not expecting children to act more mature than they are.

3. Parents need to collaborate with children so as to give them the message that their thoughts and feelings count. Parents should guide children through the problem-solving process by using active listening and "how"/"what" questions. Statements such as "seems like", "sounds like" and "I wonder...."are effective for guiding children's thoughts.

4. Parents need to create a safe and predictable home environment that can flexibly respond (not defensively react) to life's unpredictable challenges.

5. Parents need to provide structure, nurture, engagement and flexibility.

6. Parents continue to guide children with thought provoking questions and active

listening. Parent values prevail through guidance and limit setting.

7. Parents deliver consequences in a firm, consistent and loving way. Parents do not use shame or any other negative tactics when enforcing consequences (since the consequence has been pre-determined, the enforcement of it is sufficient).

8. Parents model the expected behaviors to children; e.g. when parents are stressed, they use good coping/self-care skills and do not yell (or at least catch negative behaviors, apologize and use healthy coping and communication skills to make recoveries).

9. Parents continue to keep the child's developmental stage in mind so as to have realistic expectations about the child's emotional and behavioral limitations.

10. Parents keep a "wall of separation" between adult matters and children. Parents recognize that they cannot and should not be "friends" with children until the children have adult brains (around age 25); prior to this age, children's developmental needs must be considered. Of course, parents are called to be friendly and loving (even though they are not able to be "friends" with children).

Snapshot Summary

More than anything children need and long to be in right relationship with their caregivers. Children are vulnerable and totally dependent upon parents. Parents not only provide food and shelter to protect and nurture young bodies, they are powerful influencers with the awesome task of "mapping" young human brains.

Even though the tasks of parenthood may seem daunting, parents do not have to be "perfect"; rather they need to be approachable, loving, safe, predictable, consistent and forgiving to others and also to themselves.

Appendices

Appendix A

Audio Component of this Workbook

The audio portion of this workbook is comprised of guided imagery sessions which are hypnotic in nature. Of course, this means that you are never to listen to them when driving a car or operating any type of machinery of any type (see the warning at the beginning of this workbook). It also means that you must never listen to them in any place or at any time you need to be present in your environment (whether it be needing to watch a child, a pot on the stove, need to make a phone call by a certain time or any other matter that requires your complete or partial attention). The sessions are hypnotic because they draw your attention to internal experiences; this may include: using your imagination; paying attention to your breathing (and other interior body sensations); recalling memories; and following stories that are full of metaphors for building life skills.

Hypnosis Explained

In order to understand the concept of hypnosis, it is easiest to first rule out what hypnosis is not.

Here is want hypnosis is not. Hypnosis is:

- **Not Mind Control** –You may relieved to know that you do not turn into a mindless zombie who is subject to the will of the hypnotic guided imagery session or hypnotic therapist voice. If this were true, people who are skilled in hypnosis would rule the world and any reasonable person clearly knows that this is not the case.

- **Not Sleep** – As unfortunate as it may seem, there is indeed no such thing as sleep learning. If you happen to fall asleep during a guided imagery session, you will not benefit from the concepts of the session because you will be sleeping. Your dreams can and may be influenced only by what you heard prior to going to sleep.

- **Not a Power that Overrides Your Value System** – This means that even if you volunteered to be a participant in a stage hypnosis show, you cannot be "made" to "cluck like a chicken" or anything else that is against your value system It cannot make you do anything, whatsoever, that you do not want to do (remember this is not mind control). People who participate in stage hypnosis volunteer to do so because they are revved up to do it. They want to "say yes" and want to be "good sports" and have a good time. And even when the conditions in the last sentence exist, a person can still not be made to do something goes against values or interest or will. It is true that people who are vulnerable (due to having poor personal boundaries or mental illness for example or any other reason) can be manipulated by an unethical stage hypnotist (or in any hypnotic setting) but this is also true for people in the general population in a wide variety of other settings (e.g. think of advertising, political rallies, fashion statements and so forth). During hypnosis, people can always choose to end any hyper-focused, interior state (which is what trance is) by simply saying or thinking "no" and opening up eyes (just saying "no" re-engages the executive critical thinking areas of your mind which easily overrides your imaginative thinking side).

- **Not Something You get "Stuck" In** – People cannot get stuck in hypnosis since trance is a natural state that people go in and out of in varying degrees all day.

- **Not a Belief System** – Some people insist that hypnosis is "against" their religious beliefs. When that is the case, the answer is to not participate in it. However, one needs to consider that hypnosis is not a belief system. It is a natural state that your brain goes in and out of all day long. It only requires you to narrow your field of attention and turn your focus inward.

- **Not Unconsciousness** – People are completely aware of everything that is happening around them during hypnosis since they are not asleep; they just happen to be highly focused on an internal experience (the internal experience may be a physical sensation or it may be a memory or imaginative escape). People can end hypnosis whenever they need or want to reorient themselves; however, when they are so highly focused on an interior experience (memory or day dream), they may not be as immediately attentive to the exterior situation as it warrants (hence do not listen to hypnotic material when you drive or operate machinery). Common experiences that supports the notion of not being unconscious is when people "mindlessly" walk into a room or find their way around their houses. When people are so intensely focused on a thought, it is easy to forget why the room was entered or even forget how one got there.

- **Not Just Relaxation** – It is true that many (if not most) guided imagery sessions will guide you into a relaxed and comfortable state (because relaxation facilitates focus and also feels good); however, it is not a requirement to generate the trance state. As previously discussed, people can be jogging, moving around the house or out and about anywhere while experiencing momentary or protracted trance states (which they maintain by selectively focusing).

Here is what hypnosis is. Hypnosis is:

- **Highly focused attention** – Focus and absorption are the key ingredients to creating a hypnotic state. It is a state that is usually directed inward (as when facilitated by an in-person therapist or guided imagery recording) but people can also develop trance when they are focused on some external thing that is very absorbing; e.g. a movie; TV show; a particular hobby; reading and so forth. Trance is characterized as being a state of highly absorbed and narrowed/selective focus. This is what a hypnotherapist or recorded hypnotic session attempts to do; i.e. help you focus in a highly absorbed and selective way (on the suggestions, imagery or story that is presented to help you learn the concepts/skills you desire to improve).

- **A fantastic tool for learning** – Since hypnosis is all about absorbing attention, the fact that it facilitates a person's learning process should not be surprising. Hypnosis is widely used in many areas to accelerate and strengthen skill development, cultivating positive attitudes and more. It is commonly used by professional athletes, sports teams, speakers and others who want to enhance performance (via increased focus). It is also used by major university health centers that treat chronic pain; i.e. it helps people change their focus and experience pain in different, less challenging ways. There is quite an extensive amount of research that supports the efficacy of using hypnosis to manage and reduce the experience of pain. Much of it is astounding; e.g. people who are able to undergo surgery without the use of any anesthesia because they have been trained through hypnosis to turn off any pain inflicted by the surgery.

- **More than the process of making direct suggestions** – Certainly direct suggestions (e.g. "You will quit smoking") can be of value to someone who wants to make changes that are congruent with the suggestion; however, direct suggestions are the most easily rejected type of suggestion. Permissive styles of suggestion that are in line with the person's value system are much more readily accepted. These type of suggestions include but are not limited to telling stories, using metaphors and guided imagery. Permissive suggestions allow the person's own value system to interpret and make meaning in a way that best fits the goals identified. Direct suggestions are most useful when a person has a strong ability to focus and is in strong agreement with the suggestion given (i.e. "I do want to quit smoking" rather than "My spouse wants me to quit smoking").

- **"Believed in Imagination"** – This term is widely used when therapists explain the concept of hypnosis; it was first coined by Dr. Ernest Hildegard more than 50 years ago (he is a pillar in hypnosis research) (Yapko, 2012). "Believed in imagination" is a very simple, yet apt description since it helps you understand the power of your thoughts. There are so many examples that you can consider which illustrate the transformation of energy from thoughts to changes in biology. These examples include: people begin to salivate after intensely imagining the sight, smell and taste of favorite foods; people measurably raise or lower body temperature (e.g. in one hand versus another); people "turn off pain gates" and so much more. When people give themselves permission to imagine, they give grant themselves access to the incredibly vast non-verbal, symbolic and emotional universe of their right brains (at one time referred to as the unconscious mind). This is a very powerful resource in which to tap for making all kinds of desired change. Imagination is not just "fluff" or silly or foolishness. It is the juice that motivates us; inspires us; changes us and leads us to take action inside and out. If you are still in doubt, consider how all the things you can presently see, hear or touch started as mere sparks from someone's imagination.

- **Self-hypnosis** – This is the simple truth: "All hypnosis is self-hypnosis". People focus on what they choose to focus on. Unless a person complies or gives oneself permission to day dream and go with the imaginative flow presented by a recording or in-person therapist, there is nothing that a guided imagery recording or hypnotic facilitator can do (remember there is no such thing as mind control).

Hopefully, you now have a better understanding of what hypnotic guided imagery is and is not. Perhaps you can also recognize that hypnotic imagery is very useful in breaking undesirable patterns of behavior and for learning new skills. Thus, the reasons the audio sessions have been added to this parenting skills workbook.

Being "The Good Parent" is not an easy task. In order to be a good parent, many people need to overcome the deficits of the parenting they experienced when they were children. If efforts are not made to overcome these deficits, people run the risk of passing the mistakes of one generation to the next one.

This is not about pointing fingers of blame at any particular generation; since, surely, each generation could point to the previous one. This is about recognizing and stopping dysfunctional patterns that stymie child raising efforts and inadvertently injure children. The goal is to increase the self-awareness of parents so they can make more informed, and age-appropriate decisions to guide and nurture children. Hypnosis is a great tool to help increase self-awareness, facilitate learning and change dysfunctional habits.

Skills Addressed in Audio Files

Skills Addressed in the 3 Audio Downloads

1. Life Skills - to counter anxiety and depression patterns of thinking and behaving.

2. Setting and Defending Healthy Boundaries - for discerning what one "will take and not take"; fortifying authentic identity; helps identify problems to be solved.

3. People Can Change - bolstering the notion that change is possible; even when it is hard; it is possible when one lays out and takes action steps.

Instructions for Accessing Audio Component of Workbook

The download webpage instructions can be accessed by scanning the following QR code. You will find links for the audio files as well as the transcripts for them.

http://www.screencast.com/t/toDIgVMv

Instructions for Listening to the Audio Recordings

There is no "right way" to listen. People are free to listen in any way that feels comfortable and in any way that allows them to focus, become absorbed and engage their imaginations. People can follow every word said in the recorded sessions or they intermittently pay attention to the words said. The only challenge to experiencing the hypnotic state would be when a person focuses on analyzing the words spoken instead of "going with it" and allowing themselves to have a daydream-like experience. People can also interfere with their experiences of trance by "trying too hard". This is why it is useful to "relax" and "let go"; even if these are not necessary conditions for trance to occur.

Transcript for the Life Skills Audio Recording

Life Skill Building – by Lori Olson, M.S., LCMHC, LMHC, CCHT

Better life skills and parenting skills can grow and shape you and everyone you care about...in so many ways.

And so now, you may already be learning...how very easy it really is....to begin to focus...inside....and begin to find that place....inside....that helps you to relax....so very comfortably....inside....and relax....and you can....whenever you are ready....to close your eyes....and focus inward....and find that place that deepens your very comfortable state...and I don't know where that might be....and I don't know how you....might already know....how to get there....but I do know...that it is... as easy as this....notice your breath...noticing your breath...or perhaps...for you....going to that safe....and warm memory....of lazy days.....somewhere...where somewhere is for you...perhaps sun drenched....or wet with warm waves....of anticipation...or appetite...for whatever whets...whistling a happy....comfortable...favorite tune...of yours. You can choose...whatever delights...and holds...you safely....comfortably....in a deep....and meaningful way....or whatever way **you feel...fit**

And you can listen...in anyway...you choose....and in any way that works...because you already know...that the only right way....is the way that left....all those must do....and should do ...and must be...and have to be...behind...you can...you know...be free...to listen...carefully....or go....where you need to go...in a semi-listening sort of way...to comfortably relax....deeply relax....and still listen...in whatever manner...you **need to hear and learn.**

Whatever way you choose to relax....and whatever way you choose to listen....whether that is in or out...or careful... or aware...or mindful...or present....in the here and now...you are awake....you stay awake...and you do hear....right here...right now...and **the present is the one**...two...or three down...**one gets to open**...and discover... and go...and get...and be... so much more...isn't that right? For where else can one **make change**...only in the present....the past is left....the future...gets hatched....from the present...you open today.

So whether a warm and balmy beach is where you go....or someplace...firmer...and cooler....or deeper down... that path...of very comfortable... freedom...you can go there....even as I tell you of someone... I knew...who did know too... know...how to get so very...very comfortable...and relaxed.

And so...this person... knows...how to focus....and relax....can take a walk... along a warm....and soft....sandy beach...so comfortably soft...the kind of softness...that is kind on your feet...and allows the sinking....deeper and deeper into the softness and warmth....and the waves can do 4....or 3....or two...or one lap....deepening the....very pleasant....and relaxed hold....on...you can... let go....and be more.

One knows...there are so many things...one can notice...waves on a shore... one sure thing....or another...one can feel...content... and soft caress...the sand...deep and warm...and taste the salt...water...wet...and rhythmic....balmy breeze....bathing body....mind....and spirit....free to be...deeply absorbed...in your mind...and on your mind...and so your mind...can absorb....everything it needs to know...to relax...and focus...and absorb....the very soothing...and comforting awareness...of what it means to relax....and freely be...growing....awareness...that you can be more....with self....awareness of what...and where... and how... you want to grow.

And just how does a person grow? And isn't it true? People can...and do...grow....in all kinds of ways...and means....and that means...surely... you can too. It is just a matter... of course...of knowing...which course to take...and where to start.

And that reminds me of another some...one....couple...a city couple...who yearned for more...more peace... and greater piece....of space and time...and place to do much more...so they...decided....that the right thing...meant... they left....that city...there....to find the right place...in the country...here. Oh yes...and of course...on this course...as one might... expect...they hear...a chorus...naysaying...perhaps ...well-meaning... but naysayers...nonetheless...herds of them...neighing....trampling...ideas....a couple dreams... or more...and so an uncertain one or couple...might retreat...to the safety of the known...or an uncertain one or couple...might...instead... venture out to strive...to seek....to find...rather than yield to a passing herd of thoughts....and they could....and did... ask questions and found what they need to know...that helps... ....because a couple of well-placed questions....and a mind... set to ponder and wonder....and do....can really do a whole lot more...and help this couple...or any other wonderers...to leave those who help....less...more or less behind.

So here is what they did. They figured out... what they did know...by looking...thinking...feeling...hearing...tasting...testing. They figured out what they didn't know... by looking...thinking...feeling...hearing...tasting...testing. They asked....and looked....and dug...and figured...and considered...and asked some more....and read...and heard and read....and looked and listened and twittered and followed... those who knew much more...and all the while... they started doing what they figured...and tested what they learned...and did it more...and again....and more and ever so much more....now...you may figure...that this was sort of like two steps forward....and one step back...and maybe it was....3 or 4 such one or two steps in either direction...but I can tell you...this couple changed....to what they wanted...by those steps....and all because of this...they either never heard that baloney...or at least never believed it....that life is easy....or life is always safe....they knew...and felt...and learned...what they needed to do...to make it work....to what they want....to do....to make it grow.

What worked...for them...and they told me...too...that it works...for anyone...else that is told too....and it is sort of like this...some people ...just might starve... if all they had...

was a whole elephant to eat....those people might think....the skin is too tough...the elephant is too big...or perhaps...I could never swallow it...or even...think...it is too hard to know...even if... it were the only food...for life or thought...what to do...and yet...one can...eat an elephant....you really need to know....it is true...and right on...the way...that city couple took....one bite....one piece....one part....of the whole puzzle...at a time. Sizing up the situation....figuring out....and taking on....just what they could; take on...and do for now....what made sense....and what needed more...sensitivity...so to speak...and finding out....how to serve it....up or down...in a cup or pot of whatever soup they found...or... one find's... oneself... in ...perhaps spicing it up...and making it tastier...better...healthier...longer lasting...more meaningful...more energizing...more memorable. Oh sure...they had... those bites...they kept...chewing...chewing....chewing...on....perhaps....sleeping or not...sleeping on it...or under it...that is...of course...'till they learned....and they did...how to....slice it up thinner...and they did...how to...simplify the recipe....steps 1....2... and 3...and they did...and take action...which they did....instead of...you know... swirling and chewing...around in one cooked spot...And you will be glad to know...the happy ending...in this once upon a time...is that one did and can choose how one chews all kinds of news...and one can make out of it whatever one needs...when one takes one's puzzle one piece at a time.

And so one can spin and pin this tale on any party game...or figure out that there is much more than meets the eye or ear...and one can look deeper and listen deeper....and see and hear so much more....that nothing finishes unless one starts...and nothing changes...unless one slices....or steps...or climbs...or risks...a climb or even takes a fall...because one knows....and must know those poetic words of strength....that when one falls and splats....or winter follows any fall...one can and most know...when winter comes... spring can't be far behind....and there can be a spring in your step...even after a fall....and that is when you know you are moving....really moving...and making change...and becoming something more than staying and pining...for more...you move and shake....and shakers and movers...are all that and more.

So whether one leads one or more....one can lead more...effectively...when one sizes up...slices...and dices...and serves...and tweaks...and decides what to put in...and what to take and not to take...in any kind of recipe for life...for love...for children...for business...for zest...and purpose...on purpose....for change....is what you make it...one step...two step...dance...in any way...you find...or dine...one chews.

Let's not forget... but.... remember...what that city couple....also...really.... had to do....you know ... hold up... bear down...and stand up...and take...the uncomfortable....the negative...the unpleasant feelings...that naysayers chortled...or strummed...or whinnied or whined...or neighed... in all sorts of refrains....oh...well...that couple heard that herd...and whether they liked it or not....that couple fared quite well....and are...as a matter of fact... out choosing finer fare right now.

And so...once more... there are ...so many things one can learn.....so many ways one and you can... choose ...to accept... and to respond..... **to hear and learn** ....to figure... where to set a line...and size and resize...something... and when and where... and how to slice and dice and ...when to take action...and what action one needs ....to... pay attention .....To consider......to change and grow... and so much more.

And you know it's true....that we all want first responders.....since first reactors set off all kinds of chains...that lead to somewhere else....so...you can...tone it down.....to ponder.....to wonder.....to calmly seek alternatives....that you are in a better place.....whether you move there in time....feeling....space.....mood....thought....or behavior.....all kinds of better place....and you can choose one.....when another is not the one for you......you can choose what is a better way to respond...and listen...and truly hear...and figure out...the best way... to guide you and more.

And so in the minutes......hours....days.....weeks and months to come....you can....and.... will continue to experience a growing....and profound...positive sense of change....an increasing desire to know how to do more...in more...responsive ways... because you can choose and make it so much more...and I do....and you can.... wonder how soon you will begin to notice.

And now you can choose.....to continue experiencing these increasingly empowering thoughts and feelings in trance.... And perhaps.... if you so desire....and whenever you so desire...you can...if you want.... Enjoy these experiences as you...rest and fall asleep....and sleep...very deeply and very comfortably....and feel renewed and refreshed...however...if you need to....or choose to... you can begin to experience these empowering thoughts and feelings... even more deeply right now ...and each moment of every day...with new vigor...relaxation...and self-awareness of what you can and will do to make the positive change you want and need....and you can do all this....and more...as you begin to reorient yourself to the sounds and events around you.....

Transcript for the Boundary Skills Audio Recording

Boundary Skill Building – by Lori Olson, M.S., LCMHC, LMHC, CCHT

And perhaps you know...that there are many types of boundaries...and fences that guard...and protect those boundaries...with gates one can set... to open... or close....and decide...what to take in and what to keep out.

There are all kinds of ways to relax.....and you may have already discovered some of them...afterall....it just takes a moment....to close your eyes and change your focus.....from the outside....to the inside....and I do not know where you will choose to place your focus.....perhaps....you may begin to notice....the interior sensations of the tips of your fingers.....on your right hand.....or your left .....behind....the attention....you give...you may notice that there is no right way...and all that is left is to relax....because you can relax.....that's right....you can relax.....simply....noticing.....the fingers on each hand.....and wondering when...you might begin to notice the subtle differences... between those....on your right .....and on your left ....which of those fingers may feel ever so much lighter.....or ever so much heavier....and I don't know....how you will begin to experience... those infinite subtleties that exist....all along.....but come to awareness....when you take the time to notice.....that's right.....you can leave anything you want....outside...for a moment or more....when you take the time.....to pause.....and look.....and notice.....what is relaxing.....what is here.....and now.....relaxing.....and a minute....can feel like an hour.....and an hour like a minute.....when you pause....and savor....become your story's author.... Eyes on new things....or old things in new ways.

And as you continue to focus....on how very easy... it can be... to focus on the familiar....yet oddly...unfamiliar....you might consider...as the saying goes...."knowing it like the back of my hand"....and yet ....one may or may not know the details of that hand....curious....isn't it? So as you focus.....you may find....that you can be ever so curious....as to what you will experience next. And I don't know....what you will experience next.....but I do know....that you can learn to focus.....and relax....ever so much more.

After all....you know....and I know...that the mind works in mysterious ways....and that an imagined bite of your favorite food.....when focused on.....all its flavors....and aroma.....and texture....will soon enough...lead to that mouthwatering.....desire for more.....and so...you do know....that imagination...does translate into physical action. And what runner....or athlete....hasn't turned a thought ...into physical readiness?... when the start of that games is signaled.....now...you know too....how your mind does that too....one way or another......

And so....you can begin to learn....and begin to use....your wonderful imagination.....in ways that perhaps...not imagined before.....3....2....1....deeper.....and ...deeper....relaxed.....relax......to change.....you can...relax...to change the way you approach.....you can relax into... change the way you interact.....one can you know....choose to respond.....and influence.....the way one experiences....the experience at hand......whether it is left or right.....and what is right... depends...on you....depends on...values....depends on....what type of person....one chooses to be...doesn't it?

I wonder....and you may wonder too....how one does become the person one wants to be....it seems to be a matter of fences.....rather than de-fenses....you know....where and how one boundary lies....to set a fence......and where that fence is strategically placed....in a place that makes sense....and when one places it.....such a fence....only needs to be maintained.....since all the labor goes in....one time....to figure out....where and when to place it.....it sort of reminds me of how farmers must make decisions as to where and when to put up fences to keep in sheep....and all of this....of course....depends on what type of sheep you have....and where you have them....and what sort of risks.....exist around.....farmers in Iceland....do not need many fences....as a defense for sheep.....since there are no risks.....only foxes....if one is or has a chicken....and one does need to protect....and evaluate....when there is risk....it only makes sense....to one who looks.....and figures....out what is needed.....

So sheep...at least in Iceland.....get to roam the countryside....mostly free...of fences....yet....of course....there is a price....so to speak for everything....or perhaps....tradeoff....is a better word. Icelandic sheep do protect themselves.....with wool.....thick coats.....of wool.....very thick....dense.... protective boundaries....against the elements.....the wind.....the cold.....the snow....the icy rain.....and so....a wooly defense...or fence....so to speak....all kinds....depending.....on what one needs.....and what one values.

New Hampshire sheep may benefit from a warm and cozy barn....so they....can find green pastures when the time is right.....and open the barn door....when it makes sense to invite... what is right and good....whether that be hay or grain....or a shearer....or when it makes sense to venture out....and find new fertile grounds.

And I suppose.....and you can suppose too....that setting a fence.....a boundary....of any sort....is a matter of what makes sense....so one can decide....you know....you can....decide....where and when to place that boundary.....and it goes like this....one can decide what one needs.... and what one can do... and what makes sense...and when one knows....and only when one knows these things....can one know where... and when... and what kind of fence to build....the right type of fence for the defense that is fair and true...and right....is the one that rings true for the type of sheep....or farmer....or place....or person...or thing....the only right thing is the thing that is left....when all the other unimportant things are moved away.

And so....wouldn't you agree?...That it is safe to say....that fences are only useful....

When they meet the purpose they are meant to serve. And so to keep a fence useful...one needs to maintain it....and adjust it...and strengthen or relax it... as seems right....as there is no right of way...unless it is freely given...as it is the job of any good and truly useful fence....to keep what's right in....and keep out what is left....over there.

One can always remember....that there may be times when the fence is tested....by the elements...whether it be the snow...the sun...some...driving wind...or other driving force to distraction. No matter....one can always...give a good..."oops"....to make a repair as needed.....to ponder what can be said....and done to build the fence back up. Because...isn't it true... that so much of life is actually about the repair....and having the flexibility to know when to make them....and salvage what is still good....versus starting from scratch....when you know what is worth building upon....a lot to consider.....with fence building...and people get good at what they do....and do again....and get better at it ....when they look at... and do... what works...and at what can... and does... work better.

And that of course...gates and locks work better too....when moved and used...and flexed and played in a way...that practices the standards of that fence.

This all reminds me of what it takes to learn something new.....sort of like....when one learns to play the guitar. In the beginning.....there are some decisions to make....you know....what sort of guitar to get.....6 strings or 12 strings....whether to buy or to rent the guitar....whether to self-teach.....or take lessons.....whether to practice every day....for how many minutes?....10...15....30....one can figure all these things out......and yet one never actually can learn to play the guitar....unless one...after all... does it.....takes it and figures out.....where to place the fingers....or how to hold a pick....if one is even to pick.....something....

Anything that needs to be done....needs more energy in the beginning.....time and energy into developing skill......growing skills....skills that can and will... take on even greater.. and much more... interesting....and perhaps more complex challenges...whether it be walking to running....uttering to conversing....self-regulating to socially regulating....or picking a guitar or strumming it....alone or in a band. It is....an initial investment....in energy and time....with all kinds of dividends....one can imagine...the thrill of scaling that initial mountain turned bump....and navigating the slopes with speed and accuracy....it is all a well-earned payout...born from focus....and figuring out.....and choosing.....where and when to take actions needed.....whether to make a fence....or draw a line....with a finger or a pen....play a guitar....or ski....all moguls.....know how to take one step at a time...or even get back up... to achieve something small or large....and it is all good...perhaps you already know....that good things come in small packages....but large ones too...and one can...largely know where one needs to go...but it is in the details....that is....in the steps....forward and sometimes back...that one must take... to get there.

You can take some time to reflect.....and consolidate...the knowledge...that it can take time and energy to build a strong and useful fence....and...there will always be those....times...when any boundary or fence or gate may get tested....and also times...when a good boundary or any decision...whether to let in or out ...may need maintenance... or repair... all of this....and all of that...and when you do....reflect upon it...it will come to no surprise... or any mystery...at all... and you may.. just find....a just way to apply...all of this...or some of that...to your daily life....making sense of what you need....and setting fences around the boundaries... you need and want...to make life easier...sweeter...safer....ordered....comfortable...and so much more.

And so in the minutes......hours....days.....weeks and months to come....you will experience a wonderful sense of change.....just because you can choose to make it so much more than what it is now.....and I do....and you can.... wonder how soon you will begin to notice.

So as you continue to reflect on all of this and so much more....you can take all the time you need....and only when you feel ready....you can begin to increase your awareness of the sounds and rhythms of all that is around you.....and gradually reorient yourself.....you can open your eyes....whenever you like.

Transcript for the Positive Change Audio Recording

Positive Change Building – by Lori Olson, M.S., LCMHC, LMHC, CCHT

And so....let's begin....by considering.....that...People of All size....and shape...and kind...can Change...simply... by Being Open and Discerning...and so as you begin to listen...and go to wherever you may go...as you listen...you can....feel free...to close your eyes....and relax....and wonder....as...

I wonder.....the kinds of things you may have watched.....in a fascinated sort of way......mesmerized perhaps.....by the ever changing pattern in a hot glowing coal....or log on fire....or how fire....really has so many parts....those flames....that dance.....upon the wood....I wonder....if you've ever noticed...as I have noticed.....how those flames seem....at once...separate.....and also a part....of the whole. And there are many parts to a flame....have you noticed......the dark blue part.....the bright yellow.....the orange and the red? And I read more than once....or even twice....how odd...one knows...how the blue part is the hot part....strange....to think of all the ways blue can seem....but hot is not one....that stands out....among the other two or three or four other tunes....of blues.....if you get my riff or whatever else blew in....perhaps you too have been captured by that same orange....yellow and red....this time...on a fallen note...and one can notice how such a leaf may swirl.....as it falls....and lifts...one.....two.....three times in the wind.....moving down the path.....further down....and even deeper.....to a ravine....swirling ever...ever more....as it catches that ripple...and waves back to the leaves behind.

And so the wonder goes....jiving a new rhythm....with a chorus of babble....in brooks.......watch... how that free spirit....aerialist...rips right along...now... as a raft...of course a leaf...from that page; of this tune... or autumn tree...can navigate a stream.....of motion....and look...here comes a rock to roll; over....and over to another...rock and dance around another.....flowing water and leaf....joined by beating sticks.....a rhythm of life.....and movement...and all that jazz....and no matter....what kind of weather....**one can choose**....whether one is a leaf....or a stick...or babbling to another...one can choose...to dance or sit along the bank....sit along the wall....or with the flowers.

And with all this talk about falling leaves...moving wind and water....and rhythm.... in time; in space and sound....it comes to mind....how all things do move together in a dance....of sorts.....and the how question really is not...whether one knows the steps....but **how much one is willing to learn**....and one might also wonder....**how much one is willing to work**...to **learn those steps**....when one is new....and the ground may still be hard....and unthawed....and not quite ready for planting. And so one could and can recognize....that there is a time and place for all things...so....what good does it do to fret....unless...of course....it is a matter of guitars...and that kind of rhythm....but in all else....isn't one better served....by looking at what....and where....and when....and how much....whether it is...time and energy....sowing and reaping....and one could try to rush it all....but to what avail? Since isn't it...after all....what anyone...already...knows...that new wines need to wait...and age....old tales...tell us that...no wine before its time...and one can whine and moan....and stamp and fret....but what apple ripens before a bud...and what leaf turns color and falls before a spring....into action....you might just want to do....just that....but how; then; would one be able to **smell those roses**?

I have known many people who insist that apples never fall far from the tree. And I wonder if you have heard this too...and I wonder what you think of apples....falling.....predestined apples...hmmmm....fallen since Eve;ning time.....One can look and wonder about so many things....of apples....and knowledge of apples....and trees of....knowledge...of apple trees....and how one does fall....if one is to fall....one could suppose....that a lot more goes in to it than meets the eye....know....and you do too....**that there is more than one way to raise and harvest anything....worth raising**...right?

And so...even if one is a tree....of shallow roots....weak or broken boughs....how silly to bow down... or take a lesser route...when one can always prune...or graft....or brace...and spray or fertilize...holistically...or any other way that ripens fruit to mark it right. **There is always a way to change what one needs and wants to**....will...find a way.

And you may be wondering....what all this has to do with apples....and how people are like trees....and apples....and how one could be the different one... in one's family tree....yeah...that's right...the different one...from all the rest....and even... how this might be good for some...and not for others.... Who think more like rotten apples, or sour grapes...or black sheep...if you consider animals and other kinds of kingdoms... Whatever the baaaa or batch....isn't it true....that every story begins with "Once upon a time"....at this time and place...and under these conditions....the plot does hatch....and something more is always born....whether that be fruit....or labor....or children.....the story has just begun. And everyone knows that you can't predict the weather from what happened last year or even yesterday....and so one can know...and people do know that an apple or a child is so much more than the tree upon which it rests....and whether the weather helps it....is another matter....**because apples can and do change** into all sorts of things...tart things...sweet things...sour things...healthy things...and whatever else one chooses to do with the knowledge that trees can give.

All I know...is that a wise person once said....that **the best way to predict the future**....whether that be for an apple....a rose...a sheep....black or otherwise....or even for a person**....is to create it**....here and now....and not worry about the past....it's done. And if one could change the past...one might...and others surely would...but I know and I hope you do too...that all the pining in the world can't change what's done....and so...the only things to change are those things ...that you can influence....here and now...like the way you talk...and make yourself known...the way you listen.... if you really care...and if you really hear...one's tone...or tune...or beat...or patter of little feet...It's no small feat...to be real...and vulnerable...and open...and in the moment...It is a risky business....being real...and yet....it is the best way to predict the future...being real....and open...flexible and bendable....a creator...of the future...from what was to what is...to what can be...for you...and those you love...to be more with you...more by you...more for you...more than you...more than a simple

135

measure of one's proximity to a tree.

And who knew...there are so very... many...varied... ways to view a crop of fruit...the oddest of which ...is to see one's sown fruit as products of sorts....I rather like The Prophet's take....this paraphrase... you may...already know... "Your children are not your children; ... rather...the sons and daughters of life's longing for itself... coming through you but not from you....and though they are with you yet... they belong not to you. Listen up parents...be bows... from which your children are living arrows sent"... strong stuff...wise stuff....sending forth... oh Tell...an apple....quite distant from this or that tree by any other name....whether now parent...you are a son or daughter too....**to be or not to be what you can be.**

And so the invitation is simply this ....remember well... what it is like to be small and vulnerable...and a better guide you'll be. When you're big and strong....and maybe gnarly...you may see a toll... in being vulnerable...one knows....it may not feel safe...but oh well....to **live well and prosper**...we all know... that meaning...means calculating...all choices and all risks....when responding well... choose emotional closeness...gluing....bonding and guiding ....sprouts and spouse... children...and a better you...all need limits...being heard....and herded in the right way...to the right loving and firm....age wise limits...collaboratively set... collaborative effort... shaded from the drama.... in the protection of strong....safe....predictable....fair...loving....flexible....steady...wise....competent problem-solving...even if gnarly....knowledge tree. And **how much are you willing to learn**...how much energy in time and space....can you give...to **create a better....future**....when you learn... you leave the past..... of course...this means the changes can start now ... with how and what you know....about you...and what you can do....and what you need to change...and want **to change...your way**...for the better everything....for the better everyone....for the better you....for the better **now**.

And I guess...it all depends...you know...change that is...depends....on...whether... **one accepts and uses feedback** ... sees it...hears it...digests it...feels it....as the vital input it is...to get so much more from the world...you know.. as to what this is like...or that is like....for them...for others....as it seemed....or how it sound....useful stuff...after all...the world is not just one....thin plot...or just your plot... or lot...in life....and how much more....with many plots...perspectives and points of view...much more interesting...wouldn't you say... than one size fits all....how dull...how boring...how old...how limiting...how sad...how useless...if one just pushes back what is fed...in an oversensitive....defensive...way...foolish thinker...sizing up a whole world...one way....street...a narrow street...And how much more useful it is to wonder...what that is like for you...or you...or you...small child...young teen...a parent or two...a partner...or any other... one or more...one meets...greets...shares...or sees... accepting...and making sense of feedback in a thoughtful....intelligent way. And you can do this all...even when...yes...even when and if...you hear something...and you don't agree....the feedback feed... can... be digested...used... and be useful...quite useful information... about the world...so you can know...and can figure...and can...better decide...what to do...what to say...and so much more.

Of course...one also needs to know...that anyone can toss you.... a rotten apple...or tomato...or a hot potato...or fishing line and hook....and perhaps disguise it as feedback....and so it is...that it makes sense for you...to filter feedback...sift it through....and look at....through a sense filter....set a boundary....or two....or three....or four...or more...healthy....boundaries....make sense....and you can set them...too. And one can and must easily remember.... there is no...no...no...never...ever... an excuse for abuse...whether that be...verbal or...any other...wise men and women know otherwise...no matter how packaged...even if... it is promoted or packaged... as feedback.

And so there are many things that you can learn.....so many ways you can choose to...accept and respond.....to feedback.....to figure...what makes sense...and where one needs to agree or set a boundary or ....to... pay attention .....To consider......to change and grow... and so much more. And isn't it true....that when you learn to respond.....you can...tone it down.....to ponder.....to wonder.....to calmly seek alternatives....that you are in a better place.....whether you move there in time....feeling....space.....mood....thought....or behavior.....all kinds of better place....and you can choose one.....when another is not the one for you......you can choose what is a better way to respond...and listen...and truly hear...and figure out...the best way... to guide you and more.

And so in the minutes......hours....days.....weeks and months to come....you will experience a wonderful sense of change....an increasing desire to know how to do more...in even more responsive ways...just because you can choose to make it so much more... than what it is now.....and I do....and you can.... wonder how soon you will begin to notice.

And now you can choose.....to experience these empowering and lovely thoughts and feelings in trance....or you can begin to experience them now... each moment of every day.....as you begin to reorient yourself to the sounds and events around you.....

See Appendix H for hypnosis themed exercises and handouts.

Appendix B

Brain Neuroplasticity and Hypnosis

"The brain is neither predetermined nor unchanging, but rather is an organ of adaptation." (Cozolino, 2002).

"The power of psychotherapy to change the brain rests in its ability to recognize and alter unintegrated or dysregulated neural networks." (Cozolino, 2002).

The Brain is shaped by Experience

Modern neuroscience research abundantly supports the notion that the function and connection of "neurons depend critically on experience" (Straub). This researcher goes on to say, "The brain is changing and growing continuously throughout life, shaped as much by experience as genetic heritage. The higher the level of the brain, the more it is shaped by *experience*."

Other key neuroplasticity findings:

- "Deficits in communication and neural functioning within the brain can be compensated for by the brain's plasticity, which allows the regions of the brain to *develop new neural pathways and improved communication later in life*." (Amini, Lewis et al, 1996)). This means that no matter how old you are (parent or child), you can change old and dysfunctional patterns of thinking and behaving. This is done by learning and using more adaptable; more effective; more pro-social; and developmentally appropriate communication and coping skills. These will contribute to creating healthier experiences to positively influence the brain (parents and children).

- "*Imagery activates the same regions... [in the brain]... as in vivo experience and can be used...to initiate change.*" (Straub).

- Whether the brain constructs the past, predicts the future or reconstructs the

138

past (Nadel), it is all "here and now experiences". "These constructs serve…as templates of our perception and experience… [And so]…"serve as filters to our experiences, provide emotional (often subliminal) triggers to the meanings we give to situations and trigger responses". (Straub)

- Changing the way we recall and view memories can **result in change in beliefs, meanings, emotions and behaviors** (Straub).

Since hypnosis is "believed in imagination" (Yapko, 2012) and the neuroplastic brain changes in response to imaginings and experience, one can begin to recognize the tremendous therapeutic value hypnosis has for shaping perspective, changing dysfunctional thinking patterns, processing feelings and altering problem behaviors.

Help Your Neuroplastic Brain Make Positive Change

Guided imagery and trance are powerful tools for making positive change. Here is some information that will also help you make changes in "non-trance" times of life.

The following information is taken from the Positive Psychology Program website:

http://positivepsychologyprogram.com/train-your-mind-for-happiness/hnique-for-stress/

This website offers useful positive psychology tools for mental health practitioners for a yearly subscription fee.

Can You Train Your Mind for Happiness?

A simple answer is yes. At birth, our genetics provide us with a happiness set point that accounts for about 40% of our happiness. Having enough food, shelter and safety makes up 10%. Then we have 50% that in entirely up to us. By training our brain through **awareness** and **exercises** to think in a happier, more optimistic, and in a more resilient way; we can effectively train our brain for happiness.

New discoveries in the field of positive psychology show that physical health, psychological well-being and physiological functioning are all improved by learning to "feel good". (Fredrickson B. L. 2000)

What are the patterns we need to "train out" of our brains?

1. **Perfectionism**– Often confused with conscientiousness which involves appropriate and tangible expectations perfectionism involves inappropriate levels of expectations and intangible goals. It produces problems for adults, adolescents, and children.
2. **Social comparison**– When we strive to do and be better than others rather than better than we did in the past.
3. **Materialism**– People who attach their happiness to external things and material wealth are always in danger of losing their happiness if their material circumstance changes (Carter, T. J., & Gilovich, T. 2010.).
4. **Maximizing**– Maximizers search for better options even when they are satisfied. This leaves them little time to be present for the good moments in their lives and with very little gratitude.

(Schwartz, B., Ward, A., Monterosso, J., Lyubomirsky, S., White, K., & Lehman, D. R. 2002.)

What are the patterns we want to encourage?

- **Gratitude** – a sense of reverence for things received.
- **Resilience** – the ability to bounce back from setbacks or failures.
- **Connectedness** – this can either be the sense of all being connected to one another at a level of consciousness or a sense of social connection that provides emotional support.
- **Mindfulness** – the awareness that arises out of paying attention in an open, kind and discerning way (Shapiro, S. L., Carlson, L. E., Astin, J. A., & Freedman, B. 2006).
- **Optimism** – expecting that the future will be desirable.

How our brains are "wired for happiness"

The human brain comes ready for happiness. We have care giving systems in place for eye contact, touch and vocalizations to let others know we are trustworthy and secure.

The human brain regulates chemicals like oxytocin. People who have more oxytocin trust more readily, have increased tendencies to monogamy, and a more care giving behavior. These behaviors reduces stress which lowers production of stress hormones like cortisol and inhibits the cardiovascular response to stress (Kosfeld, M., Heinrichs, M., Zak, P. J., Fischbacher, U., & Fehr, E. 2005).

We are remarkably capable of happiness if we just get out of our own ways.

Positive Psychology – core virtues

The field of Positive Psychology has identified the following 6 core characteristics that are universally valued:

- **Wisdom**
- **Courage**
- **Humanity**
- **Justice**
- **Temperance**
- **Transcendence**

Positive Psychology summarizes each of the values this way:

Wisdom – having intellectual strengths that help you gain and use information

Courage – have strengths of will that help you accomplish goals in the face of fear and also when experiencing internal or external obstacles

Humanity – having interpersonal strengths that help you befriend others and maintain relationships

Justice – having social strengths that help build a healthy community

Temperance – having protective traits that help you avoid excess and stay on track when faced with temptations

Transcendence – having strengths that connect you with the larger world and help you find meaning

Positive Psychology breaks the core characteristics down to identify the underlying strengths in each one. Below are the core values and their associated strengths:

Wisdom – *creativity* (using imagination to develop original ideas and objects); *curiosity* (feeling safe and interested in exploring new experiences); *open-mindedness* (being able to fairly look at things from other perspectives; able to change one's mind when new evidence is introduced); *love of learning* (building upon one's foundation of knowledge); *perspective* (looking at the world in a way that makes sense to you and others)

Courage – *integrity* (speaking truth and acting in an authentic way); *bravery* (thinking and acting in a way to support what you believe and not shrinking away from what threatens you (physically or emotionally); *persistence* (finishing what you start even when it is hard); *vitality* (enthusiastically engaging with life; using life energy effectively)

Humanity – *social or emotional intelligence* (being aware of your motives and feelings of others); *love* (valuing and maintaining close relationships with people); *kindness* (nurturing and caring for others; showing generosity and compassion)

Justice – *teamwork* (displaying loyalty and responsibility and working well in a group); *fairness* (treating everyone justly without being influenced by personal biases); *leadership* (encouraging others to get things done; organizing and following through; promoting good relationships among team members)

Temperance – *mercy* (letting go of grudges; forgiving); *humility and modesty* (truthfully acknowledging who you are and what you have done; letting your accomplishments speak for themselves); *self-control* (regulating what you feel and do; being self-disciplined); prudence (not taking undo risks

Transcendence – *appreciation* (noticing and valuing excellence in nature, performance, professions and everyday life); *spirituality* (holding beliefs about life and a higher purpose); *gratitude* (taking time to express thanks); *hope* (believing the future can be good and taking action to make it happen); *humor* (being playful)

Additionally, Positive Psychologists have examined each of the strengths to determine which ones most significantly contribute to happiness.

They have identified these strengths to be happiness boosters:

- Curiosity

- Vitality

- Love

- Gratitude

- Hope

Positive Psychologist Martin Seligman (2012) says that in order for people to lead meaningful lives, they should focus on building their strengths. This helps people build realistic goals that are congruent with their natural tendencies.

Studies (Seligman, 2012) showed that emphasizing a person's strengths in a job performance review gave people a 36% bump in improved performance afterwards. When weakness were emphasized on job reviews, the studies showed a 27% decline in performance followed these reviews.

Seligman (2012) invites people to visit http://authentichappiness.org to take the brief strengths assessment. You will also find questionnaires about hope, gratitude and other indicators of happiness and positivity. The assessments are free and results are provided after you complete the questionnaires. The site does require that you sign up in order to gain the results of the questionnaires.

The Positivity Ratio

According to Positive Psychologist Barbara Fredrickson, when negativity floods self-talk and decision making, it impacts your children and everyone else you encounter. It adversely impacts your physical health (see above example about heart attacks). It also impacts your body's ability to rest and restore itself. Given that negativity has such powerful impacts, Dr. Fredrickson began to wonder, more than twenty years ago, what impact having positive attitudes would have on relationships, bodies and sleep.

Dr. Fredrickson and her team of positive psychology researchers found that when people experience positive emotions in a 3 to 1 ratio to negative emotions, people begin to feel better about themselves and lead more productive lives.

Watch Dr. Fredrickson describe her new book on YouTube.

See Appendix H for neuroplasticity themed exercises and handouts.

Appendix C

Summation of the Anti-Anxiety Skills Parents Need to Model and Children Need to Learn

Anti-Anxiety Skills

1. **Recognize vague and all-encompassing global thinking**. Problems cannot be solved when they are too vague or too general. Goals cannot be reached when they are too vague or general either. It is important to look at the situation or problem in a more granular way. "I just want to be happy" is an example of a vague statement. And so is "I am in crisis". Each of these statements needs to be better defined in order to see the size, shape, scope, and character of the problems to be solved or the goals to be achieved. Action steps need to be identified and then taken to solve the problem or move toward the goal. In the case of the global statement, "I just want to be happy", the person would need to clarify what would constitute being "happy", i.e. how would it look, feel, seem (e.g. would it be as an entrepreneur; planting an herb garden; listening to children laughing; getting sober; being a beach bum, creating art projects; writing computer code and so forth). Clearly anyone of these things might represent a piece of the happiness puzzle to someone. Movement towards goals and resolution of problems can only be achieved when realistic action plans with a logical sequence of steps (including back up plans) are created (Yapko, 2012).

2. **Learn to compartmentalize**. Learn to break unwieldy, vague and global thoughts into bite size, workable tasks

3. **Learn to discriminate**. Learn to choose what to focus on and what to ignore; determine what is in or out of one's control and work on the tasks that you can

influence.

4. **Learn how to put an end to useless and energy sapping ruminations**. Identify action steps to problem-solve "what if" type worries and determine courses of action; take actions when appropriate.

5. **Develop awareness to stop externalizing.** It is important to recognize that blaming others leads one to feel helpless and hopeless. It is important to be able to discriminate (see #3) what is in and out of one's control. People need to accept what is truly out of their control and focus on any parts (compartmentalization; #2) that can be worked on, changed or improved.

6. **It is very important to learn how to empower one's self (no victims).** Research indicates that people who identify with the "victim mentality" do not experience change (Yapko, 2009). Victims feel helpless and hopeless. The victim mindset is a powerful one for getting and staying stuck. Whether the case is acute trauma or whether it is chronic trauma or whether people feel victimized by circumstances of crime or are victimized by natural disaster, people need to re-orient and find ways to take charge again. They need to develop an internal sense of control (opposite of externalizing; #5)

7. **Stop internal attributions**. Internal attributions are external "proofs" that "confirm" one is defective or incompetent or "less than" in some way. A person with an internal attribution draws conclusions about oneself from circumstantial or irrelevant external information. For example, when someone does not answer your email, you conclude that it is because the person does not like you (when there are very many other reasons for not responding to email) (Yapko, 2012).

8. **Turn against maladaptive coping methods**. Avoidance styles of coping are particular problematic contributors to the creation of anxiety. People who use avoidance types of defenses typically have very low distress and frustration tolerance. They use avoidance to "escape" the unpleasant sensations stemming from triggered fight/flight/freeze responses. Unfortunately, the actual problem which triggers the negative feelings never gets addressed when avoidance defenses are used (e.g. anger signals someone has "crossed your boundary"; fear signals danger; sadness signals loss has occurred; and guilt is your own evaluation that you did not do something according to your standards). Thus an avoidant person will feel anxious and stuck (which leads to depression) because problems do not get resolved.

9. **Build a sequence of logical action steps that lead to your goal** (Yapko,

2009). Action is an important antidote to anxiety and depression. Well thought out action is very empowering. People who take steps toward a goal feel much happier with their lives (Csikszentmihalyi, 1990); even when the goal is challenging and hard to reach. People who learn how to accept feedback so they can appropriately and flexibly revise action steps demonstrate resiliency (Seligman, 2012) and are more likely to achieve their goals.

10. **Determine whether expectations are realistic or not.** If expectations are not realistic (e.g. "becoming an award-wining singer" when one cannot sing in tune), then it is important to revise expectations in order to create obtainable goals (e.g. working in the music industry in a non-singing capacity).

This skills are not only important for eliminating psychological experiences of anxiety and depression. Consider that positive psychologists found that people who had experienced a heart attack were more likely to have a second heart attack in the next 1 -8 years when they continued to use "blame" tactics in daily life. People who learned from their experience (in this case the heart attack) and began appreciating life more were much less likely to have a second heart attack (Seligman, 2012).

See Appendix H for anti-anxiety themed exercises and handouts.

Appendix D

Additional Healthy Life Skills for People of All Ages

1. Good Impulse Control

2. Ability to Regulate Emotions (via self-regulation and social regulation)

3. Developing an Internal Locus of Control (building a "can do" attitude)

4. Recognizing what is in or out of one's control

5. Flexibility (ability to receive feedback and make appropriate adjustments if needed)

6. Ability to Set and Defend Healthy Boundaries in a Pro-Social Way

7. Ability to Make a "Repair" (own up to mistakes and adjust appropriately)

8. Actively Listen to the Feelings of Another Person (without trying to fix it or them; rather attune and guide with "how" and "what" style questions; this reduces emotional isolation and increases social connectedness)

9. Ability to Tolerate Frustration and Other Feelings of Distress (and recognize how to care for one's self in order to maintain one's ability to respond and problem-solve)

10. Ability to Access, Identify and Express One's Legitimate Needs, Wants and Feelings in a Pro-Social Way (having an authentic voice; this means being self-aware and in touch with one's core values)

11. Ability to Discipline Self (so as to do as one says and do what one intends to do; even when this is something challenging or inconvenient to do; such a person is not at the mercy of "whims" or "moods", can so can trust self and can be trusted by others; and can create and follow plans of actions towards goals)

12. Ability to Critically Think (this means being able to ask and consider if something makes sense and whether more information needs to be gathered to be able to make an informed decision; this includes identifying "red flags" in relationships).

See Appendix H for life skills themed exercises and handouts.

Appendix E

What Children Need – structure, nurture and engagement

Children Need Parents Who:

1. Address children's needs and feelings in timely, loving, nurturing way

2. Work to create safe and predictable home environments (both physically and emotionally)

3. Provide age-appropriate rules and consequences in advance of infractions

4. Consistently and lovingly enforce rules with consequences (and do not negotiate or explain when delivering consequences)

5. Collaborate with children to create rules and consequences; all the while guiding children through active listening and "how" and "what" questions

6. Recognize that children are "not little adults" and that it is unfair to treat them as if they are adults (this means giving children age-appropriate tasks and responsibilities; parents speak to children in an age-appropriate manner; they do not "over-explain; they have age-appropriate expectations for their children)

7. Keep adult matters separate from children

8. Show flexibility and model competent problem solving

9. Know how to admit mistakes and make repairs (especially in relationships)

10. Are not perfect and do not need to be "right" at all costs

11. Model impulse control; emotional regulation; self-discipline; pro-social communication; respect for others (includes respecting other people's boundaries and making a repair when boundaries are crossed; includes not laughing at, ridiculing or dismissing the feelings of others; even when there is no agreement)

12. Have goals and know how to work towards them (includes personal, professional and relationship goals)

13. Can create a healthy, loving family narrative (even when life circumstances are difficult)

14. Know how to cope and take care of their own needs

15. Can play, sing, dance, love, learn (spend quality time together; this is more important than quantity)

Appendix F

Core Emotions versus Maladaptive Defenses

Core Emotions

1. **Restorative** – When core emotions are expressed, people return to their "center point". People are neither distressed nor overly exuberant. For example, tears are vehicles for releasing stress hormones that build up during sadness. Crying helps restore people to a calmer state.

2. **Memory filing system** – The strongest memories are those that are "tagged" with strong emotions. Events that are not associated with any emotions are typically not remembered very well or at all.

3. **Motivation** – Core emotions provide the "juice" that drives us to accomplish things; move toward goals; create things

4. **Inform** – The various emotions signal a variety of meanings that are useful for deciphering problems and identifying the actions that are needed to resolve them.

   a. Anger – signals a boundary crossing has occurred

   b. Sadness – signals a loss has been experienced

   c. Fear – signals danger is lurking

   d. Guilt – is negative feedback telling you to reevaluate your actions

5. **Call to Action** – emotions "fire" people up with energy so they take action to resolve problems identified in #4. The call to action created by negative core

feelings often feels distressful and hence gets noticed. The inability to tolerate this distress can lead people to take impulsive, reactive or defensive actions in order to quickly discharge the energy of the "call to action". Others try to "stuff it". People who can regulate the distress are better able to respond by directing the energy of the "call to action" towards resolving the problem flagged by the emotion.

Maladaptive Defenses

1. **Misguided attempts to discharge the "call-to-action" energy** – The energy from negative emotions feels too distressful to tolerate and is released through defensive tactics such as : attacking others (e.g. yelling, sarcasm); self-attack (e.g. calling self "stupid" and other put down remarks); avoidance (e.g. procrastination behaviors; substance abuse) and withdrawal (e.g. removing oneself from others). The energy is discharged in a "non-productive" way since it is not used to effectively solve the problem that triggered the call to action in the first place.

2. **Divide or Destroy** – Instead of solving the originating problem, maladaptive defenses misuse the call to action energy and end up creating rifts in relationships or hurting other people.

3. **Indicate that there is something to protect** – Defensiveness indicates that there is a wounded or vulnerable person that does not know how to address the problems at hand.

4. **Defensiveness often looks like aggressive or like less-than-social behaviors** – These undesirable behaviors typically exacerbate and/or muddy problems instead of solving them.

5. **Maladaptive behaviors** – contribute to and exacerbate anxiety and depression experiences.

The Importance of Core Emotions

It is important for people to be in touch with their core emotions. Core emotions arise from the non-verbal portions of the brain. These include: the amygdala, brain stem and limbic regions of the brain.

Core Emotions for Survival

Core emotions have their origins, in human development, as primitive survival signals. Negative emotional signals are meant to alert people about possible threats that exist in their environments. Positive emotional signals alert people about opportunities for bonding. Since people are social creatures, this also is about survival.

In general, core emotions alert people to the size, scope and nature of a situation in the environment that may impact or assure safety. Core emotions are natural and mapped out of the experiences that a person has in life.

Core emotions are triggered when neurons that were previously "wired together," in response to a combination of stimuli (i.e. sight, smell, sound, touch, taste), are "fired' again in the present moment. "Wired together" neurons are very sensitive to environmental cues.

When a person has experienced trauma in the past, the brain becomes extraordinarily sensitive to "wired together" cues. No matter how "irrational" the stimulus appears to be, the brain is just doing its job; i.e. trying to assure survival. This is why it is foolhardy for parents to "police emotions". Instead, parents need to help children learn how to respond to their core emotions. This will help them build and "fire" new, more adaptable "circuits".

Investigate Alarms to Disarm Them

People need to be responsive to what they feel since this is the healthy way to receive and read the message that is being generated by the non-verbal portions of the brain. When an emotional message is "read" by the executive centers of the brain, the "call-to-action" charge is reduced and the person can choose the best course of action to solve the problem that has been identified.

"Reading the message" is what happens when a parent guides a child using active listening questions. "How" and "what" questions help both the child and parent understand what the emotional signal is trying to convey. In the case of anger, this may mean that a boundary of some sort has been crossed. In the mind of a two year old, this boundary crossing may be that "you put me in the car seat when I still want to play". In such a case, the child's resistance is about feeling a loss of choice and not about the car seat at all. When parents "read the message" they can better solve such a problem by offering the child a couple of choices; e.g. "Would you like to take this toy with you or would you rather take this book?" Giving the child choices restores the

154

child's sense of personal power and lowers the resistance to the car seat (which was not the problem at all).

Adults can actively listen to their own feelings by asking themselves the same "how" and "what" questions. They can also explore their own feelings and help their children explore feelings by thinking or saying "seems like... X" or "sounds like...X".

Using Emotional Maps

During childhood, emotional mapping of the brain helps people wire the physical experience of feelings and the verbal descriptions of those feelings together (see workbook section on child development). People can access emotional maps by using "seems like...X" or sounds like...X" type of statements. When someone is able to describe the feeling in a way that "rings true", then the feeling has been accurately identified.

The person who identifies the feeling is now better able to identify the problem that underlies the emotion. Identification of a feeling with words helps move the non-verbal emotions to the logical executive centers of the brain. This is the area of the brain where problem-solving occurs. This means the person is now better set to begin problem solving.

It is All about Survival

It is not easy for many people to tolerate the physical sensations precipitated by emotional "calls to action". This is because emotional "calls to action" arising from negative feelings are experienced as distressful. They are distressful in the same way that physical pain is distressful. Nonetheless, both types of sensation, physical pain and emotional pain, are useful, because they get your attention and inform you about things you need to know.

The physical sensations caused by triggered negative emotions are "fight", "flight" or "freeze" survival responses. These responses include: increased heart beats; sweaty palms; rapid breathing; queasy stomachs and so forth. The more intense the emotions, the more intense the physical sensations will be. These sensations are automatic and will occur whether people acknowledge their feelings or employ maladaptive defenses to ignore their feelings.

When people ignore or block feelings, the "call to action" is still felt but experienced as random and mysterious rather than connected to a problem to be solved. "Calls to action" might be experienced as generalized anxiety that inexplicably invades a person's life or they may lead to behaviors that seem aggressive, edgy or inappropriate in a variety of other ways. "Calls to action" are meant to be heard so their charge can be dissipated and the source problem be addressed. When emotions are ignored, the "calls to action" are not dissipated but continued to be unpleasantly experienced in the body. This creates a high baseline of internal distress (a.k.a. anxiety).

Misguided Coping

People learn to employ maladaptive defenses for a variety of reasons. These include: not learning to tolerate and manage the distressful physical sensations of the "call to action" or thinking that core emotions and behaviors are one and the same. For example, "Anger equals yelling and therefore I am not allowed to be angry" or "I am a bad person if I get angry". Maladaptive defenses also form when a child has been inadvertently told that feelings are not "okay" and they feel guilty, ashamed or defective when these feelings get triggered.

When the above reasons happen, children learn that it is safer to avoid or suppress their feelings. Maladaptive tactics such as this do not make the emotions go away. People just lose touch with them and consequently themselves. "Call to actions" need to be identified in order for the charge to be reduced and the intended message to be considered "read".

Emotional Brain Training

Dr. Laura Mellin began developing Emotional Brain Training in 1979 when creating a program to address the drive to overeat in young adults suffering from obesity (Mellin, 2010). The program evolved into a treatment that helps children and adults self-regulate more effectively. It provides very useful tools for changing the "habit circuits" that people learn and develop since the early days of attachment style formation. The premise behind Emotional Brain Training is it is "not who you are" but "what you do". People can change what they do and do not need to feel stuck with being "less than" or "defective" (the types of conclusions drawn when one negatively evaluates and blames self). Mellin's Emotional Brain Training is based on the following principles:

1. All people have 5 brain states

    a. Brain State 1 – Joy

        i. Abstract Cognitions

        ii. Joyous Emotions

        iii.   Intimate Relationally

        iv.   Optimal Behaviors

   b. Brain State 2 – Good or Balanced

        i.   Concrete Cognitions

        ii.   Balanced Emotions

        iii.   Companionable Relationally

        iv.   Healthy Behaviors

   c. Brain State 3 – Mixed

        i.   Rigid Cognitions

        ii.   Mixed Emotions (positive and negative)

        iii.   Social Relations Level Maintained

        iv.   Moderate Behaviors

   d. Brain State 4 – Becoming Unbalanced

        i.   Reactive Cognitions

        ii.   Unbalanced Emotions

        iii.   Needy/Distant Relations

        iv.   Unhealthy Behaviors

   e. Brain State 5 – Irrational

        i.   Irrational Cognitions

        ii.   Terrified Emotions

        iii.   Merged/Disengaged Relations

        iv.   Destructive Behaviors

2. All people go in and out of these brain states; the degree that one experiences negative brain states depends on the number and strength of maladaptive defenses that are used (see above section on maladaptive defenses and core emotions).

3. Brain State 4 is considered to be an "opportunity for change". Emotional Brain

Training research has found that Brain State 4 has enough emotional charge to "open up" the brain's neuroplasticity (so that circuits can be changed) and also just enough cognitive capacity to make more informed choices (i.e. instead of reacting one can still choose to respond; even though it may feel distressful and hard to do).

4. Brain State 5 is the land of the "runaway train". The imagine conjured up is that of a train losing its breaks, careening out of control down a mountainside while its freight cars are fully loaded with coal. A person in Brain State 5 experiences being out-of-control behaviorally, emotionally and cognitively (even if inside the person is thinking…. "Oh no…what am I doing/saying"). It is an ugly, debilitating state that leaves carnage to self and others. It ruptures relationships and sometimes (depending on the level of behaviors) even causes physical damage. Brain state 5 is such a highly reactive and dysregulated state that it becomes important to train brains not to go there.

5. How does one not go into a Brain State 5? The answer is by putting the brakes on (while one still has them) in Brain State 4. It is important to stop the "habit" that has developed (or may yet develop) of going into a Brain State 5 since Brain State 5 feels and is so destructive to self and others. Brain State 5 contributes to people feeling shame since it is the "proof" of one's defectiveness (this is what people think in the aftermath when the carnage is reviewed).

6. According to Dr. Mellin, recent studies in neuroplasticity support the notion that people can change their brains; no matter what the age. The notion that "you cannot teach an old dog new tricks" stems from the reality that the longer a habit is cultivated, the harder it is to change. Because old habits require more insight about what to do to make change happen and because persistence in doing the tasks to make change is required, people wrongly conclude that change is not possible after a certain age. The 2 major factors that impact whether a person will make effective change is whether or not the person believes "that is just the way I am" (and therefore is helpless to make change) and whether a person takes adequate measures (including persistence) to make the changes.

7. Emotional Brain Training is based on "emotional plasticity". It offers behavioral tools, when repeatedly used, mirror the "evolutionarily-based secure attachment between parent and child" (Mellin, 2011).

8. Emotional Brain Training helps people "rewire" their brains through activation of the maladaptive circuit (i.e. the maladaptive defense reaction) and altering

the experience from being reactive to being responsive and calming down. This contributes to the alteration and reconsolidation of the circuit. "Similar forms of treatment that reconsolidate allostatic circuits have been published for obsessive compulsive disorder" (Mellin, 2011).

Rewiring the stress response: A new paradigm for health care. (2011.). Retrieved September 21, 2015.

See Appendix H for core emotions and maladaptive defenses themed exercises and handouts.

Appendix G

Attachment

There are now so many amazing studies in neuroscience that inform us about how the human brain becomes organized at birth and beyond. Researchers no longer believe that infants have no ability to make meaning of their worlds. On the contrary, they now realize that it is their "job" to make sense of the world and the people in it. They do it in a way that seems completely foreign to older and more complex thinkers. Infant brains use sensorimotor input and rely on impressions to make sense of it all.

And of what are they trying to make sense? Infants need to figure out how to have their needs adequately met by their caregivers. Their very survival depends upon learning how to signal hunger and comfort and how to get relief. This meaning-making process continues throughout childhood.

Successes and Challenges

The degree to which infants' efforts are successful or challenging ultimately influences the way they perceive the world. Does the world present as responsive and safe or indifferent and distressful? Does the infant have to put a lot of energy into having needs heard and met? There are so many variables that can and do influence the way infants make meaning of their worlds.

When the meaning infants make is that the world is hostile or that they are helpless, infants can become "apathetic, depressed and withdrawn" (Tronick & Beeghly, 2011). 2011). Infants who feel threatened may become "hypervigiliant and anxious or hyperactive...others develop rigid or dysregulated patterns of self-regulatory behavior or have difficulty making sense of themselves or others". These can..."distort how infants master age-appropriate developmental tasks, such as developing self-regulation, forming attachments with caregivers or establishing autonomy." Researchers also state that "aberrant meanings amplify and heighten infants' vulnerability to pathological outcomes".

Matters of Attachment

The experiences children have, even very early ones, color the way they interact with the world. Early experiences inform the meanings that children make about the world and about themselves.

Do children feel that the world is safe enough to take the risk of exploring it? This is called having a "secure attachment". Insecure types of attachment may be described as avoidant, ambivalent and disorganized styles and arise out of the types of experiences children have with their caregivers. Only the secure type of attachment will:

> "...enhance the likelihood that infants will acquire more resources from their exchanges with their caregivers in the short run, and these growth-promoting interactions will, in turn contribute to resilient outcomes in the long run. In contrast, infants with harsh, unresponsive caregivers may learn to minimize their engagement with the caregiver in order to safely maintain proximity with her....Although this avoidant behavioral style may be adaptive in the short run, it may increase the risk of long-term maladaptive outcomes, such as a tendency to form insecure attachment relationships with others later in life" (Tronick & Beeghly, 2011).

Experiences Matter

The research shows that it is really important to provide safe and predictable environments, not only during the infant stage of development (which is foundational) but through all stages of child development. Experiences do matter. They influence emotions, behaviors and even gene expression.

Appendix H

Handouts and Group Exercises

Hypnosis

Sample Hypnosis Consent Form for Practitioners

Hypnosis Agreement

Informed Consent to Do Hypnosis

I, _____ acknowledge that the process of hypnosis has been explained to me. I understand that hypnosis uses guided imagery to focus thoughts and to build psychosocial skills. Hypnosis also involves the use of indirect and direct suggestion as well as metaphors to help develop the needed skills outlined in my therapeutic treatment plan.

I recognize and accept that hypnosis is not sleep and is not mind-control. I recognize that I am free to end trance if at any moment I choose to do so; for any reason; whether I feel stress or no stress.

Hypnosis has been described to me as "believed-in imagination" which means that I must be an active participant in order for the process to exist. I understand that this essentially means that all hypnosis is "self-hypnosis" and that the therapist is simply facilitating the process while providing suggestions/imagery that are congruent with my therapeutic goals. I understand that I should report to my therapist any expectations of having to testify in a court of law, since my therapist will advise me not to participate in hypnosis until my testimony has been made (so as to prevent any dismissal of testimony; e.g. false memories).

If/when the therapist provides me with a recorded hypnotic guided imagery

CD/AUDIO DOWNLOAD, I agree to never listen to the CD/AUDIO DOWNLOAD while driving a car or operating any machinery or during any activity that requires me to be alert. I understand that the guided imagery CD/AUDIO DOWNLOADs are hypnotic in nature and that it would be hazardous to listen to them in any place that is not safe and comfortable and appropriate for being inattentive to surroundings. I also confirm that I do not have any disclosed or undisclosed medical conditions that would contraindicate the use of hypnosis.

When I accept a CD/AUDIO DOWNLOAD, I also understand that I am not to share the CD/AUDIO DOWNLOAD with anyone else; since the CD/AUDIO DOWNLOAD is provided by my therapist as a part of my therapeutic program. I agree to be responsible for the use of the CD/AUDIO DOWNLOAD by anyone or in anyplace that does not meet the terms of this agreement.

Signature of Client   Date

_____   _____

Printed Name of Client

_____

Parent/Guardian Signature   Date

_____   _____

Self-Hypnosis Instructions

The "Betty Erickson Self-Hypnosis Technique" is a very popular technique that is described on many websites throughout the internet.

The following resource is from:

Betty Erickson Self Hypnosis Technique for Stress (Hypnosis and NLP Blog Hypnosis Training and Self-hypnosis Techniques RSS)

http://trancedout.com/blog/betty-erickson-self-hypnosis-technique-for-stress/

"This technique was developed by Betty Erickson, who was the wife of Dr. Milton Erickson who we all know and love. Although Dr. Erickson's wife was not a hypnotist per say, she did have an understanding of how our representational systems (visual – auditory – kinesthetic) impacted our world, and the trance state."

"This is a great technique that she came up with, that has become very popular. This can be used for releasing stress or any other type of self-hypnosis that you'd like to do."

"Before you begin the process and slip into self-hypnosis, you may want to set goals for what you wish to have happen, or to go over the suggestions that you wish to circulate when you are in the hypnotic state. When you are ready, follow these steps."

The Betty Erickson Self-Hypnosis Technique for Stress

"Step 1: Become comfortable
Sit or lay down in a quiet and comfortable place. Relax your mind and body and feel yourself beginning to drift into a state of calm soft relaxation. Let yourself go inside slightly while remaining aware of the outside world and having your eyes open but beginning to become sleepy.

Step 2: Concentrate on something that you are seeing
The shadows moving across the wall, or the unique patterns of the environment can provide something unique for you to see. Notice what you see and become aware of it. Do this three different times, with three different items.

Step 3: Concentrate on something that you are hearing
This could be the sound of your breathing, the wind brushing up against the windows, or the hum of the air conditioner. Find three different things and notice them and let them into your awareness.

Step 4: Concentrate on something that you are feeling
Maybe it's the movement of your muscles along-side the joints, the space between your shoulder blades, the weight of your feet on the ground, or the heaviness of your body in the chair. Notice three things and become aware of them.

Step 5: Continue with two things, and then one thing
Repeat steps 2-4, and this time see two things, hear two things, and feel two things. Then do the same for one thing.

Step 6: Close your eyes and go inside
Allow yourself to go inwards and become relaxed, and feel yourself drifting ever so slightly. This is a calm peaceful state where you can just let go.

Step 7: Imagine a new or old sight
This could be what you saw beforehand, or it could be something completely new. Imagine something that you can see. Maybe it is a purple elephant, maybe it is a calming blue light, or maybe it is the sight of a boat taking off from the harbor.

Step 8: Imagine a new or old sound
You can either make up a sound or it could be something already known to you. An example is you could hear a sound of an animal in the wild, or of a space ship hovering in outer space, or of soothing rain falling upon a group of leaves.

Step 9: Imagine a new or old feeling
Become aware of something that you had noticed before, or perhaps something that you wish to pay more attention to, for example how your breathing feels as it enters

your lungs, and the relaxation around your collarbone as you breathe out.

Step 10: You are now in hypnosis!
In this hypnotic state you can give suggestions to yourself or simply relax and let the suggestions take effect that you had in mind before you began the session. Simply trust that your mind is letting the suggestions circulate – the more that you can let go, the easier it will be for your suggestions to take root inside.

Step 11: Emerge
Tell yourself "As I count from 1 to 5, I will emerge with a great sense of energy and excitement, feeling refreshed and relaxed." Then count up from 1 to 5, allowing all the time that your body needs to make that true for you."

Group Hypnosis Exercise

Therapists may use the following script in a group setting. Participants are invited to sit in a comfortable position and listen in any way that feels right. This means people can listen to every word, every other word or just let their minds go to wherever day dreamy states lead. There is no wrong or right way to listen; although the best trance states exist when the participant gives one's self permission to let go and experience the imagery (rather than analyzing it). The closing of eyes helps to facilitate an internal focus.

The script is best read by the facilitator in a natural, relaxed and conversational pace. There is no need for a "perfect" reading to elicit the experience of trance.

Exploring Parts

Written by Lori Olson, M.S., LCMHC, LMHC, CCHT

I know that sometimes it is difficult to relax

Or learn how to relax more than you have before

And so, as you sit there with your eyes closed, and begin to become aware of your own thoughts,

Of your own sensations,

I begin to wonder if you have ever had the pleasure of sitting on the bank of a river or on the shore of a lake or ocean.

Because there is something very comforting about just sitting there, listening to the peaceful sound of the waves, as they move in and out, in a continuous flow, that just seems to go on and on and on.

Relaxing in the sun, feeling the soothing warmth and just letting the mind drift effortlessly with that quiet...almost silent, sound, in the background of awareness.

I'm not even sure....you've ever done that before, relaxed in that way, listening to the peaceful quietness of water washing the shore....

Perhaps it was a waterfall, or just a silent place in the woods, a happy memory of contentment or just a dream...of a place so comfortable and safe...that it was easy to allow the body to relax, everything to relax. I don't know but I do know that everyone has a place they can go, a relaxing space deep down inside where they can really let go of all their cares and concerns and wonder at the wonder of those waves of relaxation, at the smooth heaviness of arms and legs as relaxation continues.

Maybe it was the warm smoothness of the soft white sand, you could hold in your hand and watch flow effortlessly through your fingers, the same sand that flows in an hourglass, hour after hour, with nothing to do for a time except let go and flow, warm, heavy sand, listening to the waves of relaxation, secure inside and out, while you were sitting there, by the shore forgetting to make the effort it takes even to try to be aware of when or where that relaxation began and the soothing sounds or sensations were.

And as you find that safe, relaxing place....you may happen to recollect and gaze upon the shore....wondering perhaps....at the wonderful way the waves continue to meet the land....creating a shoreline.....and one sure thing about that shore.....I am sure you know....is that it takes two to make it happen.....without the waves.....and their reliable movement.....greeting and meeting.....there would indeed be no shore.....without the land....there would be no rendezvous....to have....it does take two. And I wonder....and you may wonder too.....if breaking waves....are ever being cheeky.....or snide....or even sarcastic to a shore that just has to take that fallout. After all....what can an inviting beach do? Perhaps.....taking it is enough....for now....but even rugged coastlines get worn down......and beaches erode. Perhaps it is a good thing then....that even a rogue wave....can figure out....how to be right for surfers and settle down....to be.... Just right for gentler types....and children....so all can swim and play and be tossed in a fun way and be safe.... And everyone knows...that there... are...indeed... many ways to wave.

And it takes two for more things than this shore thing......two to tango....two to court.....two to care for each other....in ways that no one .....person can do.....and how much sweeter....it is to share.....to let down the fences...or open a gate...when the time is right...or clean a garage....or fix a closet....or make a repair....any kind of repair....whether the kind you hammer, or glue, or sweep or hold or kiss...after all.....the waves need to reach the land to make it shore.....and two opposite hands are made to fit just right....and so you have it....the holding is so much more....and one can and should be whole but can be so much more....for indeed the whole is so much greater than the 2 or more parts....and there are all kinds of parts...that make the whole.

And one can be a part from something or very much a part a something....I wonder what you would choose......this reminds me of the time when I looked and saw... some who were apart and some who took part... there were some little boys and girls....perhaps 8 or so year olds... playing soccer in a grassy field.....that field was newly mowed....and still had clumps of grass strewn across... that field... of vision. There was a fresh scent from that new cut grass... still hanging in the air. The sun warmed the lazy....heavy air.....making some lazy.....and dreamy.....and slowing others down. As I watched those players... playing.....my eyes were drawn to one player...just doing one's own thing.....apart from the team.....just kicking clumps of grass...sort of oblivious to the play down the field.....no matter ....just doing one's own thing .....Fine for now.....safe...at least...'til the play moved down field... I wondered what kind of act would follow.... A player caught unaware...perhaps....would fumble... or move into action....become a part.....or stay apart.....I wondered...and you might wonder too....what choices exist....if one is not completely distracted by sweet grass drying in the sun ...or any other agenda that might be only one's own.

And who knows....perhaps that little boy or girl....had a critical voice in that head.....that took a whole "can" of cannot... and whole load of doubt....and placed doubt...on some prominent shelf....smack in the middle of the living room....of that one's mind... about how well one can or cannot play....right there...smack in the middle of mind...in this matter....the voice may say... "you are"... different... you are not...**good at more things** than kicking grass...or **good at more things** than figuring out...or **good at more** than listening to some teller....or some...disembodied voice...somewhere...some teller...who said...what you should do or not do...or perhaps...just perhaps... protecting you....or just checking out...in an ever cautious...or perhaps too cautious way.

And isn't it interesting...that a critical voice...plays a critical part...in anyone... and everyone...in one or other role one might play...or at least try to play...And I wonder...as you may too...what part in that game...or any game... or in that role or any role... it plays...in your theater... or arena...whether it be soccer......or in a team...or in a partner...or parent...or nurse...or caretaker...of oneself or in oneself. Because wouldn't you suppose....that any play writing author...you write... writes a play... with **parts that play some role**...call it a critical voice or by any other name...that role is written in... to that play... to play a that part...and one can wonder... what part it plays...how important is it...or what it serves...to play...and how it can or needs to be re-written... in some more useful sort of way. This is no child's play...indeed... some author...eyes on some purpose...brilliant stroke...perhaps...Misguided...perhaps... Overzealous...perhaps... that too...some writer...laid down...some lines or role... or part in your act...to act...to play...to what end? Everyone knows... that even minor players....in any league or chorus... contribute to... and make a line up....right...you know...a chain...is only as good as...its parts... of....who you are...

And everyone...especially any writer or editor...worth some salt...knows how to pepper a fish tale... or two...and they can...and you... certainly can and do... know too...how to spice it up...or tone it down...a notch or two....Because....after all....any overzealous spice of life ...can make a plate too salty... to consume or to make any sense at all....And any role a voice...critical or not... does play...in your play...or chorus...or kitchen style editorial ...whether....theater critic...food critic... critic of food choices or over salting critic of any other choices or other walks in life....one needs to remember...that there is that thing... about too many cooks in the kitchen...and it really makes a difference to have the one chef...and be the one chef in charge....no matter how important and how many sous chefs you have.

And I wonder....and you can wonder too... how many critics...in general....make a part of your whole...so many...all kinds... .... of ways and all kinds of critics...loud ones...sharp ones...nagging ones...dull ones...bossy ones...overbearing ones...the kind that creep out of the past...the ones that seem to silence you...the kinds that seem to reduce you....and perhaps seem to even beat...you... down...under it all...you can bet there are more critics than meet the eye, ear....and throat...hold on you...can and must know......that there are indeed...all kinds of critics.... And critics form a part...outside and inside this world....and in your...outside and inside world too....and the piece of this part....that you can give you peace ...is that even critics have a piece...you know...a part to play... in any kitchen or act...to protect....the flavor and flare of a story... or recipe for health.. and good life...to help you be what you are meant to be...And so....any critical part is so much more... than meets your eye...and one can see... when one looks...and asks...what purpose...what role...toasted...buttered...fresh or sweet...or other...wise role... does it serve in your kitchen....and how do you let cooks... serve rolls or any other food for thought you need ...and tone them down...when you need to keep all that cooks in line...

Because....as you can see...all parts contribute to the whole...and parts...all serve a part....and the whole is so much greater than the parts that serve it....and it really is just a matter of knowing how to lead...those parts... into a cohesive....and well-seasoned chorus...that is not dominated...or bullied...by one spice or voice or another...but where every voice has its part....and gets to be heard...and...importantly... ring true.

You can choose.....now.....take whatever time you need to consolidate.....and to make sense
Of what you need to do.....you can take your time..... To reflect.....and consolidate

Because there are so many things that you can learn.....so many ways you can choose to respond.....to play.....to ignore....to pay attention to.....to consider......to relax...to invite....to share... and so much more. And isn't it true....that when you learn to respond.....to tone it down.....to ponder.....to wonder.....to calmly seek alternatives....that you are in a better place.....whether you move there in time....feeling....space.....mood....thought....or behavior.....all kinds of better place....and you can choose one.....when another is not the one for you......you can choose what is better...and how to make it serve better...whether one is a food critic...a rogue wave...or just kicking grass.

And so in the minutes......hours....days.....weeks and months to come....you will experience a wonderful sense of change.....just because you can choose to make it so much more than what it is now.....and I do....and you can.... wonder how soon you will begin to notice.

So as you continue to reflect on all of this and so much more....you can take all the time you need....and only when you feel ready....you can begin to increase your awareness of the sounds and rhythms of all that is around you.....and gradually reorient yourself.....you can open your eyes....whenever you like.

Neuroplasticity and Attachment Handouts

Questions for discussion about the impact of experience on the brain

Adversity

How would you define adversity?

_____
_____
_____
_____
_____
_____
_____
_____

Are there any benefits to experiencing adversity? How does adversity impact children versus adults?

_____
_____
_____
_____
_____
_____
_____
_____

How does trauma impact people? How does it impact adults versus children?

_____

_____

_____

_____

_____

_____

_____

_____

Why does adversity seem to break some people and not others? What can experiencing adversity reveal about a person?

_____

_____

_____

_____

_____

_____

_____

What is the danger (if any) of parents over-protecting children from adversity?

_____

_____

_____

_____

_____

_____

_____

What is the danger (if any) of parents insufficiently protecting children from adversity?

_____

_____

_____

_____

_____
_____
_____
_____

Do you think people must endure some sort of adversity to realize personal growth?

_____
_____
_____
_____
_____
_____
_____
_____

Since memories are "fluid" (i.e. influenced by the situations, emotions, and cognitions that exist when they are retrieved), how can parents help children create healthy and cohesive life narratives?

_____
_____
_____
_____
_____
_____
_____
_____

How can parents prevent negative events from contaminating the way children view life stories?

_____
_____
_____
_____
_____

How can parents help children cope more effectively if crisis strikes?

_____
_____
_____
_____
_____
_____
_____
_____

"In the midst of winter, I finally learned that there was in me and invincible summer"
– Albert Camus

Positive Experience

The field of Positive Psychology has identified the following 6 core characteristics that are universally valued:

- **Wisdom**

- **Courage**

- **Humanity**

- **Justice**

- **Temperance**

- **Transcendence**

How do you think parents can effectively help children internalize these universally valued characteristics? Consider the principles discussed in the workbook. How would the framework for parenting help children learn the universally valued characteristics?

_____
_____
_____
_____
_____
_____
_____
_____
_____
_____
_____
_____
_____
_____
_____
_____

What principles from the parenting framework described in the workbook will help children build the strengths that are closely linked to happiness (gratitude, hope, vitality, curiosity and love)?

_____
_____
_____
_____
_____
_____
_____
_____
_____
_____
_____
_____
_____

_____

_____

Exercise for cultivating gratitude:

Write down three things which you were grateful for each day and describe why you were grateful. Do this for at least three weeks.

Try this right now and see what (if any) impact it has on the way you feel.

_____

_____

_____

_____

_____

Exercise for cultivating kindness:

Make a deliberate effort to do three acts of kindness each day during the next two weeks. Do them without telling anyone about your intention. Notice how you feel about doing the acts of kindness. Notice how you feel after doing them. How do you feel after two weeks of daily kindness?

_____

_____

_____

_____

_____

How can parents help children learn these strengths (modeling, telling, and explaining)?

_____

_____

_____

_____

_____

How can parents use their strengths to develop realistic goals for themselves and their children? How can parents help children build on their strengths?

_____
_____
_____
_____
_____

When you have access to the internet, visit: http://www.positivityratio.com/single.php to take Dr. Barbara Fredrickson's Positivity Ratio test. Were you surprised at the results? Discuss your findings with others.

_____
_____
_____
_____
_____

Anti-Anxiety Handouts

How does the tactic of "blame" impact the way one views the world? What impact does it have on a person's emotional and physical health?

_____
_____
_____
_____
_____
_____
_____
_____
_____
_____

Give 5 examples of global thinking (may be positive or negative global thoughts).

_____
_____
_____
_____
_____

Break up into pairs and listen to your partner's global statements. Ask your partner "how" and "what" questions to compartmentalize these statements.

_____
_____
_____
_____
_____
_____
_____
_____

_____

_____
_____
_____
_____
_____
_____

Help your partner begin to "discriminate" the above compartmentalized parts and determine what will lead to problem solving and what needs to be ignored.

_____
_____
_____
_____
_____
_____
_____
_____
_____
_____
_____

Give 5 examples of using an "internal attributional" style.

_____
_____
_____
_____
_____
_____
_____
_____
_____
_____

Use this feedback model to break "internal attributional style". Take one of your partner's examples from the previous exercise. Ask "how" and "what" questions to determine "what evidence exists"; "what inference is being drawn" and "what impact this inference has". This will help the person with the "internal attributional style" to become more aware of the faulty logic that is being used to draw conclusions.

_____
_____
_____
_____
_____
_____
_____
_____
_____
_____

Describe a logical sequence of action steps for some familiar task to you but possibly unknown to a foreigner to this country (or planet). See how many steps you can make towards completion of the goal in 60 seconds.

_____
_____
_____
_____
_____
_____
_____
_____
_____
_____
_____
_____
_____
_____
_____
_____
_____
_____
_____
_____

_____

_____

_____

_____

_____

_____

_____

Healthy Life Skills for All Ages

Consider the life skills in Appendix D. See how many of these skills go into developing the core value strengths described in Appendix B. Discuss your ideas with your partner.

_____

_____

_____

_____

_____

_____

_____

_____

_____

_____

_____

_____

_____

_____

_____

_____

_____

_____

_____

_____

_____

_____

_____

_____

_____

_____

_____

_____

_____

Repeat the above exercise with the list of things that children need (structure, nurture and engagement). How will meeting these needs contribute to the strengths needed for creating happiness? For creating other core characteristics?

_____

_____

_____

_____

_____

_____

_____

_____

_____

_____

_____

_____

_____

_____

_____

How important is it to be willing to be misunderstood? How important is it to be able to risk failure?

_____

_____

_____

_____

_____

_____

_____

_____

_____

_____

Emotional Brain Training Exercise

Emotional Brain Training (Mellin, 2015) necessitates experiencing the affective qualities of Brain State 4 in order that maladaptive defense circuits can be "open" and responsive to change. Brain State 4 also has sufficient rational cognition existing and this will influence the positive changes that are needed to change the circuit before it "reconsolidates" (see Appendix F for more details).

In this exercise, it is thus useful to vividly recall a time when you had a Brain State 4. In the privacy of your mind, see if you can remember your emotions, your body sensations, what was said and done and any other sensations (sight, sounds, taste, touch, smell) that will help you "relive" the experience in your mind. In real time, a person would actually be in a Brain State 4 and would therefore skip this part of the exercise.

Once you are sufficiently aware of the emotions and bodily sensations (fight, flight or freeze reactions) you can begin to help your mind make changes by simply listing (in the privacy of your mind) all the things about which you are: 1. Angry 2. Fearful 3. Sad 4. Guilty (do not proceed to the next emotion on the list until you have exhausted creating the list of things you feel about the preceding emotion).

When you have completed your internal venting and listing all the things for each emotion, you may notice that you have already calmed down. At this point, you may consider what is the "unrealistic expectation" (i.e. what "should" do you have) that is "driving" the maladaptive defensive reaction of Brain State 4? You need to look at it in a curious and interested fashion (no judgments that will "whip you up" again).

When you have happened upon your "unrealistic expectation" it will "ring true" and you will feel calmer again. This is the time to use humor to exaggerate and make the unrealistic expectation "larger than life" (e.g. "in the history of the world....no one has been a perfect parent....until I arrived....I am the one who....out of all the people whoever walked the earth needs to be perfect" and so forth as seems fitted to your particular unrealistic expectation).

The next step is to "step back" and consider what actually is a realistic expectation (e.g. "I do not have to be a perfect parent....I just need to be "good enough" and not afraid of making repairs when needed" etc.). Once a realistic expectation has been identified, you need to consider what action steps you will take to further your expected outcome. When you are at this point, your "circuit" will be calm and you will have made progress in changing the maladaptive one. Eventually, with repeated practice, the maladaptive circuit will become very weak and possibly become extinguished.

Rewiring the stress response: A new paradigm for health care. (2011.). Retrieved September 21, 2015.

References

Amini F., Lewis T., Lannon R., et al: Affect, attachment, memory: contributions toward psychobiologic integration. Psychiatry 1996; 59:213–239

Arnold, C., & Fisch, R. (2011). *The Impact of Complex Trauma on Development*. New York: Jason Aronson.

Betty Erickson Self Hypnosis Technique for Stress (Hypnosis and NLP Blog Hypnosis Training and SelfHypnosis Techniques RSS) http://trancedout.com/blog/betty-erickson-self-hypnosis-technique-for-stress/

Booth, P., & Jernberg, A. (2010). *Theraplay: Helping Parents and Children Build Better Relationships Through Attachment-Based Play*. San Francisco, California: Jossey-Bass.

Bowlby, J. (1988). *A Secure Base: Parent-Child Attachment and Healthy Human Development Reprint Edition*. Basic Books.

Carney, C., & Manber, R. (2009). *Quiet Your Mind and Get to Sleep: Solutions to Insomnia for Those with Depression, Anxiety or Chronic Pain*. Oakland, California: Harbinger Publications.

Cloud, H., & Townsend, J. (1992). *Boundaries: When to Say Yes, How to Say No to Take Control of Your Life*. Yates and Yates.

Cozolino, L. (2002). *The neuroscience of psychotherapy: Building and rebuilding of human brain*. New York: W. W. Norton & Company.

Csikszentmihalyi, M. (1990). *Flow: The Psychology of Optimal Experience*. New York, New York: Harper and Rowe.

Fredrickson, B. (2009). *Positivity: Top-notch research reveals the 3-to-1 ratio that will change your life*. New York: Three Rivers Press/Crown.

Gendlin, E. (1978). *Focusing*. Bantam Books.

Greenberg, L., & Watson, J. (2005). *Emotion-Focused Therapy for Depression (1st ed.)*. American Psychological Association.

Hayes, S. (2005). *Get Out of Your Mind and Into Your Life: The New Acceptance and*

Commitment Therapy. Oakland, California: Harbinger Publications.

Herschfield, J., & Corboy, T. (2013). *The Mindfulness Workbook for OCD/AUDIO DOWNLOAD: A Guide to Overcoming Obsessions and Compulsions Using Mindfulness and Cognitive Behavioral Therapy*. Oakland, California: New Harbinger Publications.

Heller, L., & Lapierre, A. (2012). *Healing Developmental Trauma: How Early Trauma Affects Self-Regulation, Self-Image, and the Capacity for Relationship*. Berkeley, California: North Atlantic Books.

Levine, P. (2010). *In an Unspoken Voice: How the Body Releases Trauma and Restores Goodness*. Berkeley, California: North Atlantic Books.

Lillas, C., & Turnbull, J. (2009). *Infant/Child Mental Health, Early Intervention, and Relationship-Based Therapies - A Neurorelational Framework for Interdisciplinary Practice*. New York: W.W. Norton & Company.

Linehan, M. (2015). *DBT® Skills Training Handouts and Worksheets (2nd ed.)*. New York, New York: The Guilford Press.

Mashek, D., & Aron, A. (Eds.). (2004). *Handbook of Closeness and Intimacy*. Mahwah, New Jersey: Lawrence Earlbaum Associates.

Mellin, L. (2010). *Wired for joy: A revolutionary method for creating happiness from within*. Carlsbad, Calif.: Hay House.

Najavits, L. (2002). *Seeking Safety - A Manual for PTSD and Substance Abuse*. New York: The Guilford Press.

Narang, David. 2014. *Leaving Loneliness: A Workbook: Building Relationships With Yourself and Others*. Encino, California: Stronger Relationships, LLC.

Nathanson, D. (1994). *Shame and Pride: Affect, Sex, and the Birth of the Self*. New York, New York: W.W. Norton & Company.

Oaklander, V. (2007). *Windows to Our Children*. Gouldsboro, Maine: The Gestalt Journal Press.

Penzel, F. (2000). *Obsessive-Compulsive Disorders: A Complete Guide to Getting Well and Staying Well*. New York, New York: Oxford University Press.

Piaget, J. (1950). *The Psychology of Intelligence*. New York, New York: Routledge.

Rewiring the stress response: A new paradigm for health care. (2011.). Retrieved September 21, 2015.

Seligman, M. (2012). *Flourish: A Visionary New Understanding of Happiness and Well-being*. Simon and Schuster.

Siegel, D. (2010). *Mindsight: The New Science of Personal Transformation*. Bantam Books.

Singer, D., & Revenson, T. (1996). *A Piaget Primer: How a Child Thinks; Revised Edition*. New York, New York: Plume.

Straub, J. (2015, March 31). TP2: Precision Cognitive Therapy: An Integrative, Deep Structure, Hypnotic Approach Helping People Modify Beliefs, Behaviors, Emotions and Existential Meaning in Life. Retrieved August 31, 2015, from http://www.asch.net/Portals/0/PDF-content/Annual Mtg Handouts/TP2-PrecisionCogTherapy-Straub.pdf

Sweezy, M. (Ed.). (2013). *Internal Family Systems Therapy: New Dimensions*. New York: Routledge.

Szymanski, Jeff. *The Perfectionist's Handbook: Take Risks, Invite Criticism, and Make the Most of Your Mistakes*. Hoboken: John Wiley & Sons, 2011. Print.

Ten Have-De Labije, Josette, and Robert Neborsky. *Mastering Intensive Short-Term Dynamic Psychotherapy*. London: Karnac, 2012. Print.

Tronick, E., & Beeghly, M. (2011). Infants' meaning-making and the development of mental health problems. *American Psychologist,* 107-119.

Van der Kolk, B. (2014). *The Body Keeps the Score: Brain, Mind, and Body in the Healing of Trauma*. New York, New York: Penguin Group.

Wilson, T. (2004). *Strangers to Ourselves*. Harvard University Press.

Wilson, T. (2011). *Redirect: Changing the Stories We Live By*. Little, Brown & Company.

Winnicott, D. (1964). *The Child, the Family, and the Outside World*. Penguin Paperback Books.

Yapko, M. (2009). *Depression Is Contagious: How the Most Common Mood Disorder Is Spreading Around the World and How to Stop It*. New York, New York: Simon and Schuster.

Yapko, M. (2011). *Breaking the Patterns of Depression*. Random House.

Yapko, M. (2012). *Trancework: An Introduction to the Practice of Clinical Hypnosis* (4th ed.). New York, New York: Routledge.

Yapko, M. (Ed.). (2013). *Brief Therapy Approaches to Treating Anxiety and Depression*. New York, New York: Routledge.

Acknowledgements

I deeply appreciate all the support and generosity provided to me by my family, friends and colleagues; they have contributed in so many ways to the making of this workbook.

My gratitude is extended in particular to the following people:

Donna Hamilton, a valuable and wise FNM&M

Deborah Olson, a very enthusiastic promoter of making dreams real

My son Ryan and my daughter Kelley for their resiliency and love

My step-daughter Lisa for surviving and thriving beyond the trials and tribulations common to step-families

My lifelong friend Lorraine Hawkins who seriously models "attunement"

My colleagues and mentors Paul Belvitch, LMHC and Audrey Williams, LCSW for their seemingly endless interest in talking "shop", sparking ideas and providing feedback.

My colleagues and friends at 50 Pleasant St. Special thanks to Rosie Traynor, MA, my very much appreciated practice manager who keeps things smoothly working. Also special appreciation for the energy and creative thinking of Denise Leville, Ph.D.

And appreciation of Franklin's perception that nothing is too big to handle; Ducky's contentment in doing one's own thing; and the fact that Dusty sometimes likes me ;)

Author

Lori Olson is a private practice psychotherapist licensed in New Hampshire and in Florida. She presently practices in Concord, New Hampshire. She is a member of the American Association of Christian Counselors. Therapeutic sessions are offered to individuals, couples and groups. Customized hypnotic guided imagery recordings are available upon request for individuals, couples and workshops. Training sessions for therapists are also available.

Comments and questions may be sent to: Lori@ADPtherapy.com

Http://ADPtherapy.com

www.ingramcontent.com/pod-product-compliance
Lightning Source LLC
Chambersburg PA
CBHW080701110426
42739CB00034B/3356